FIRE DANCERS IN THAILAND'S TOURISM INDUSTRY

FIRE DANCERS IN THAILAND'S TOURISM INDUSTRY

Art, Affect, and Labor

Tiffany Rae Pollock

SOUTHEAST ASIA PROGRAM PUBLICATIONS

AN IMPRINT OF CORNELL UNIVERSITY PRESS   ITHACA AND LONDON

First published 2024 by Cornell University Press

Library of Congress Cataloging-in-Publication Data

Names: Pollock, Tiffany Rae, author.
Title: Fire dancers in Thailand's tourism industry : art, affect, and labor / Tiffany Rae Pollock.
Description: Ithaca [New York] : Southeast Asia Program Publications, an imprint of Cornell University Press, 2024. | Includes bibliographical references and index.
Identifiers: LCCN 2023045584 (print) | LCCN 2023045585 (ebook) | ISBN 9781501774928 (hardcover) | ISBN 9781501774935 (paperback) | ISBN 9781501774942 (pdf) | ISBN 9781501774959 (epub)
Subjects: LCSH: Tourism and the arts—Social aspects—Thailand. | Affect (Psychology) in the performing arts—Social aspects—Thailand. | Affect (Psychology) in the performing arts—Economic aspects—Thailand. | Fire twirling—Social aspects—Thailand.
Classification: LCC G155.T5 P65 2024 (print) | LCC G155.T5 (ebook) | DDC 331.7/6191593—dc23/eng/20231026
LC record available at https://lccn.loc.gov/2023045584
LC ebook record available at https://lccn.loc.gov/2023045585

Contents

Note on Language

Many of my interactions with fire dancers were in the English language (or a mix of Thai and English), as many are fluent speakers. Particular Thai words and phrases were sometimes used frequently or invoked to communicate an idea, a mood, or a concept. I've included these words and others that help to communicate the particular experiences of fire dancers and the context in which they work. The transcription system used in this book is generally based on the Royal Thai Transcription System published by the Royal Institute of Thailand. Occasional exceptions are made when spelling words already in popular usage and/ or in tourist publications. In citations of another author's work, that author's spelling of Thai words is used. Pali spellings have been used for some Theravada Buddhist concepts.

FIRE DANCERS IN THAILAND'S TOURISM INDUSTRY

FIRE DANCERS IN THAILAND'S TOURISM INDUSTRY

It is the period just before sunset when the sky is softly illuminated. There is a glow in the atmosphere that marks the transition between daytime and nighttime economies on the southern tourist islands. The light hangs in the sky as the daytime heat settles, holding on while it gently sweeps away the final tourists who begin to walk back to their accommodations to shower and prepare for the evening. During this short interlude, laborers savor moments sharing food with friends before the intensity of the beach nightlife washes in. As the last slivers of light fall behind the waves, the beaches turn on: DJ'd music fills the sky and reverberates off cliffs framing darkened sand beaches; lanterns are lit and flicker in the trees; and servers, cooks, and bartenders dash from table to table to get organized as tourists reemerge from their rooms ready for the nightlife.

In the darkness, young men with fuel cans, batons, hoops, and chains walk from roads and pathways, moving through the open-air bars and into the shadows of the beach to prepare. They set up their equipment hidden by the trees. Unseen in these early moments, fire dancers will soon emerge in an explosion of light and excitement as the focus of the crowd turns to the beach. In perfect time with a loud rumble of bass from the DJ, brightness heats the skin and illuminates the ocean. The sweet, oily smell of kerosene wafts through the crowd as men burst forth from the darkness, bodies alight from fire reflecting on skin. Swirling flames color the sky against a soundscape of house music, and tourists take in the experience of fire art from beach loungers and giant pillows as they smoke shisha (flavored tobacco) and drink buckets filled to the brim with M150 (Thai energy drink), alcohol, and soda.

Sweat-soaked fire-dancing bodies twist and contort. Muscles flex as they control ropes, chains, and sticks aflame. Some dancers twirl batons as others stack themselves into multiperson pyramids while their arms continue to spin fire around their bodies. The dancers jump apart, and the formation collapses as one fire dancer runs down the beach to catch a flaming ball from the sky. The audience yelps in delight, and tourists stand in their chairs, moving their bodies to the music. Once the audience is fully hyped, two dancers walk around with a large tip bucket, and the audience is eager to give as the DJ continues the set. Other dancers carry on casually playing with fire, and the crowd moves closer to the dancers on the unmarked sand stage. The lines between audience and performers dissipate as tourists leave their chairs and tables to join, providing a natural end to the show and the beginning of a party that will continue into the early morning hours.

Fire shows are a ubiquitous part of the tourist industry on the Southern Thai islands. Employed by bars and event organizers, dancers typically perform in teams of eight to ten and work for tips or small stipends. Performances at large beach bars can be elaborate with multiple sets over an evening, while smaller venues might have only one or two dancers and a more laid-back atmosphere. What all shows have in common is their function—to sate tourists' desires for fun, excitement, and abandon—and to generate income for bars. Dancers provide a visual spectacle through performance, but ultimately they work to create feelings that are tailored to space, time, and crowds. This is not only done through their nightly shows; a significant part of their job involves mingling with tourists throughout the evening to ensure they will stay at the bar and continue to spend money. Fire dancers hone their movement aesthetics over years of daily practice, and they also develop highly skilled methods of interacting with tourists and engaging imaginaries of Thailand as happy, free, exotic, and erotic. Fire dance in Thailand is part of the affective economy of tourism (Cabezas 2009); it encompasses the management of feelings and the creation of a sense of closeness through emotional labor (Hochschild 2003) and using bodily aesthetics to produce a "liveness" that is consumed by audiences (Srinivasan 2011). This liveness—the sensations and ephemera of movement—is central to fire dancers' labor and worlds. The energies of their dance are taken in and experienced by tourist audiences. Affect is also a nexus through which dancers wrestle with the entanglement of their art form with neoliberal capitalist tourist economies and social narratives that position them as deviant beach boys rather than artists.

This book is an ethnography of the affective worlds of fire dancers in Thailand's tourism industry and it builds a theory of affect that is culturally contextualized and based on fire dancers' understandings. Affect is explored here as a bodily experience that can encompass feelings expressed as emotions and fleeting

FIGURE 0.1.   Fire dancers, Koh Samui.

FIGURE 0.2.   Fire dancers, Koh Samui.

vibes and intensities that lay below consciousness. What is the "force" of affect in this scene (Rosaldo 1989)? That is, what does affect *do*? Examining how fire dancers employ energies through dance and in their everyday lives gives insight into how they manage their identities, build communities, and negotiate the precarity and possibilities that are generated in tourist economies. Affect is a mechanism through which dancers reimagine their lives and engage the political.

Fire Art: Mapping the Scene

I saw Thai fire art for the first time in 2010 on Koh Samet, a small island located off the coast of Rayong province in the Gulf of Thailand. I was intrigued with how an artistic form I associated with European and North American rave cultures found its way to the Thai beaches and became an iconic performance. Oral histories relate that Thai fire art emerged from flow art, a movement practice brought to Thailand by backpacking tourists in the 1980s and 1990s.[1] Flow art centers on finding a smooth, rhythmic bodily flow through the manipulation of objects, often called toys, such as batons, *poi*, hoops, and chains. It draws on a wide range of culturally specific movement forms such as Maori *poi*, rope javelin from Chinese martial arts, and Hawaiian *hula*, for example.[2]

The name of the movement practice relates to Mihaly Csikszentmihalyi's (1990) conceptualization of "flow" in which one reaches a state of intensive concentration that can be pleasurable and enhance well-being. Fire art ignites flow art by using accelerants on the toys that, when manipulated by flowing bodies, create fiery traces against the night sky. While it can be a performance genre, in which artists perform in front of an audience, flow art is noted for its participatory history and ethos whereby groups of people gather to flow together, and it is often learned through informal jam sessions and community networks. Discussions with the first Thai fire dancers highlight how the form developed from, and increasingly fostered, connections, encounters, and friendships between Thais and tourists through the sharing of moves. Today, fire art is more widely viewed as a Thai performance genre among tourists, and it is fully integrated into the market economy.

The tourism industry in Thailand varies greatly in terms of geography and activities—tourists enjoy camping and trekking in the ruggedness of the North; ecotourism in national parks; cultural heritage visits to temples and ancient cities across the country; relaxing on beaches in the South; and navigating the *khlongs* (canals) and markets amid the bustle of Bangkok. Fire art is foremost an island genre catering to young international tourists partying at beach bars. This ethnography centers most prominently on Koh Samui and Koh Phi Phi,

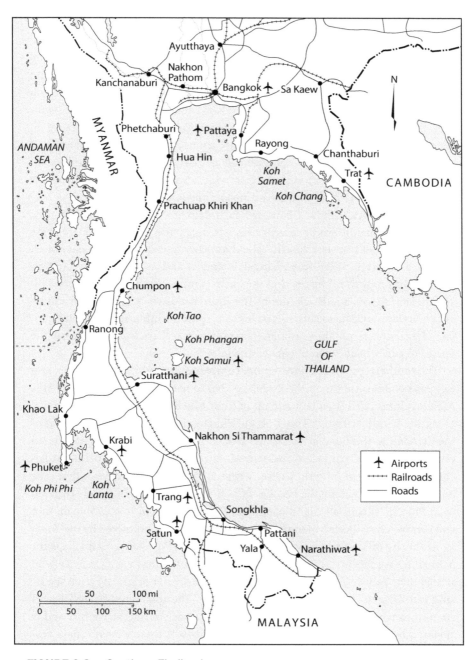

FIGURE 0.3. Southern Thailand.

with shorter durations of fieldwork on Koh Phangan, on Koh Lanta, and in Bangkok.

In the Gulf of Thailand, fire dancers perform for tourists on the following islands most prominently: Koh Samet, a three-hour trip from Bangkok and popular with expats and young Thais; Koh Chang, a small island south of Koh Samet and close to the Cambodian border; Koh Samui; Koh Tao; and Koh Phangan, the home of Thailand's famous Full Moon Parties. The infrastructure on these islands varies, although they all have a variety of luxury and lower-end accommodations. Getting to the islands is not easy and typically involves air, train, and/or road travel as well as a ferry ride. However, Koh Samui, which is the most developed island, also has an airport and is a hub in the gulf, especially for high-end travel. Samui's Chaweng Beach strip has a large mall, a Starbucks, multiple McDonalds, and expensive resorts lining the beach. There are some spaces for budget travelers, but the island mostly supports international hotels, resorts, and private villas. Koh Phangan is smaller and less developed than Koh Samui and tends to fill up around the various moon parties, such as the Full Moon, Half Moon, and Black Moon. The Gulf Islands work together on a tourist schedule around these parties, and locals prepare for influxes from Koh Phangan. Fire dancers on these islands sometimes travel back and forth on the ferries to perform at different parties and bars.

The southern provinces have a more complex ethnocultural, linguistic, and religious composition than the Buddhist Thai of nationalist imaginaries.[3] This Muslim-dominated area is made up of Thai Muslims and *Chao Le* who live alongside Buddhist Thais.[4] Tiny Koh Phi Phi Don is among the most famous of the islands and was popularized by the 1998 movie *The Beach*, which was filmed on nearby Koh Phi Phi Leh. Considered a tourist mecca in Thailand, it has become widely known for wild parties with multiple fire dance shows that take place each evening along the beaches of Loh Dalum Bay. Often simply referred to as Phi Phi, this small island in the Phi Phi Island chain is walkable on foot and completely dedicated to tourism. Prior to 1987, a year promoted by the Tourist Authority of Thailand as Visit Thailand Year, Phi Phi was a small village inhabited by approximately eighty families, many of whom were *Chao Le* who settled there to fish. Today, almost all inhabitants are not originally from the island but came to work in the tourist industry. The remoteness of the island chain means that transporting anything there takes considerable effort and is at least a two-hour boat ride. At the time of fieldwork, there were no chain restaurants on Phi Phi Don because of the issues transporting food there, although a McDonalds has since opened. Tourists flock to Koh Phi Phi Don for the parties, so it tends to be dominated by young backpackers, but many also go to visit Maya Bay on uninhabited Phi Phi Leh, a protected area where *The Beach* was

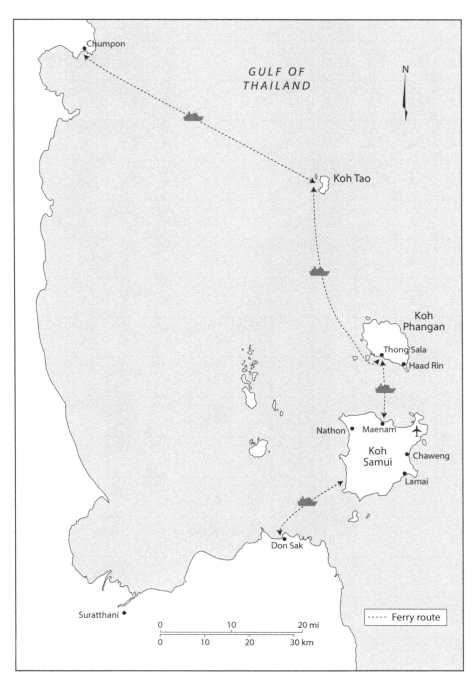

FIGURE 0.4. Popular tourist route through the islands in the Gulf of Thailand.

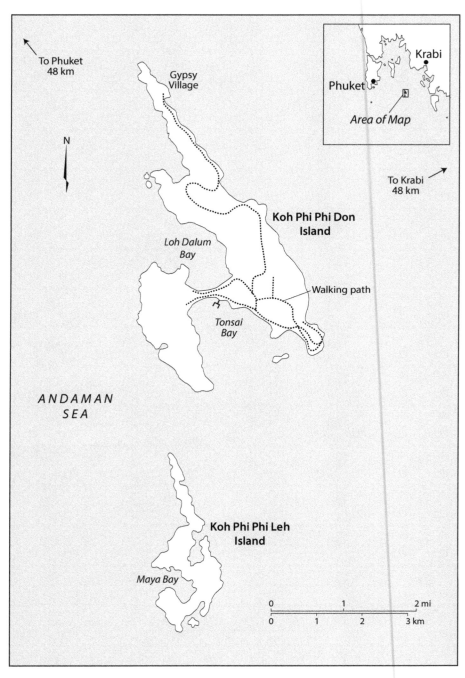

To Phuket
48 km

N

Gypsy
Village

Krabi

Phuket

Area of Map

To Krabi
48 km

**Koh Phi Phi Don
Island**

*Loh Dalum
Bay*

Walking path

*Tonsai
Bay*

*ANDAMAN
SEA*

**Koh Phi Phi Leh
Island**

Maya Bay

0   1   2 mi

0   1   2   3 km

FIGURE 0.5.   Koh Phi Phi Leh and Koh Phi Phi Don.

filmed. A short ferry from Phi Phi is Koh Lanta, a quieter island with a large Thai Muslim community. Koh Lanta has less of a party industry and, thus, less of a fire dance scene. Aside from Koh Phi Phi, Krabi and Phuket, Thailand's largest island, also host fire shows. Like the fire dancers in the Gulf, performers along the Andaman Coast also travel around these areas to dance.

Fire art performances are found in many tourist contexts around the world; what is particular in Thailand is that it is very much a male art form. Dancers are typically young male migrant workers between the ages of twelve and twenty-five who move to the tourist islands from rural areas in Thailand's Northeast to seek employment in the tourism industry. Fire dancers are increasingly coming from the neighboring country of Myanmar and are often called the new generation among Thai dancers. A foundational narrative among Thai fire dancers in what is referred to as the first and second generations revolves around how the art form lost its participatory nature as it moved into the market economy in the 2000s; this shift is said to have hindered the sense of sharing and connectedness across lines of social difference that developed as people exchanged moves and knowledge. Thai fire dancers frequently lament the increasing competition that has accompanied fire art's move into market exchange. This story was told to me by every Thai fire dancer I spoke with; it is rich with nostalgia and longing for moments that were less saturated with the seduction of capitalism and desires for economic gain.

Their sentiments not only point toward changing performance motivations but also coincide with the explosion of Thai fire dance shows across the islands in the late 2000s. This acceleration accords with a sharp intensification of tourism since 2009 when Thailand began to expand its market into Russia and China and orient the industry more toward mass-packaged tourism (Kontogeorgopoulos 2016). More bars were developed, and there was an increased need for laborers across the industry; most of these positions were filled by underpaid migrant laborers from surrounding countries, most prominently undocumented laborers from Myanmar. The Burmese formed the largest group of migrant laborers at the time of fieldwork and were mostly employed in low-paid and precarious industries such as construction, service, and fishing and farming and entered the country through informal channels (Pholphirul and Rukmnuaykit 2010).

Young men from Myanmar working near tourism areas, sometimes through luck and unanticipated connections, secured positions as fire dancers that offered greater freedom and better pay. Their precarious status means that Burmese dancers work for very low wages or only for tips, and it has become increasingly difficult for Thai dancers to secure gigs at bars. Longtime Thai fire dancers have been forced to work for less money or have been pushed out of the industry altogether. Since 2010, the scene has shifted dramatically and, unbeknownst to tourists, most fire dancers providing entertainment on the Thai islands are Burmese.[5] This shift has created competition within the fire dance scene, igniting long-standing social and geopolitical tensions between Thai and Burmese people that have existed for centuries. Despite the ethnonational differences that divide the scene, dancers share a similar trajectory into the art form. Most come to tourist areas from their home villages in search of income and work as servers or in the construction industry. Many become fire dancers through a mix of serendipity, friendship, and persistence. Performing as a fire artist on the beaches is a highly sought-after job because of the tips dancers receive from tourists and the freedom they have to participate in the transnational beach scene in ways that other jobs do not allow.

The labor of fire dance goes beyond the nightly performances and incorporates a range of affective work to keep tourists entertained. Between performance sets, dancers engage with tourists to make sure they stay and spend money at the bar. This labor might involve friendly discussion, playing games, and even drinking and partying with tourists. Unsurprisingly, these interactions sometimes result in the formation of friendships, sexual intimacies, and romantic relationships that may last days, months, or even years. While there are most certainly a wide range of intimacies that take place, those that are most publicly visible and discussed are fire dancers' relationships with *farang* (foreign) women.[6] These liaisons play on a complex mix of colonial histories and tourist imaginaries of Thailand as a space of erotic adventure and abandon and are fueled by the desires of tourists and dancers to expand their communities and experiences.

Imaginaries of Thailand

Tourist imaginaries of Thailand are filtered through an orientalist and sexualized gaze that harkens back to Thailand's being a "rest and relaxation" zone for US troops in Vietnam (Jackson and Cook 1999). The Thai government attempts to counter sexualized representations by carefully controlling the country's external presentation. It uses what Peter Jackson (2004) refers to as the "regime of images": interactions, images, and representations in the public realm are highly curated to shape a particular version of Thailand. In the context of international tourism, the government has sought to draw attention away from the sex industry. Thailand has been heavily promoted as a place for cultural tourism since the 1980s, and more recently, a carefully packaged notion of Thai culture—"Thainess" (*kwam pen thai*)—has been marketed by the Tourist Authority of Thailand (TAT) (Sakwit 2020). Thainess is a mechanism of national identity that highlights uniqueness and coalesces around a loyalty to monarchy, religion (Buddhism), and nation in ways that gloss over vast ethnic, religious, and linguistic diversity in the country. However, the TAT's "Discover Thainess" campaign, launched in 2015 in an effort to boost international tourism after the 2014 military coup, foregrounds a particular experience of Thai culture based on what it views as seven key essences of Thainess: food, arts, ways of life, wellness, festivity, wisdom, and fun (Wadeecharoen et al. 2020).

There have been concerted efforts to shift the modalities of international tourism. The industry has diversified, and the country is now promoted as a destination for medical tourism as well as a spiritual mecca. Growing international markets complement a bustling domestic tourism industry. This emerging travel practice started being promoted after the devastating floods of 2011 with marketing that reinforced Thai identity through nostalgia (Suntikul 2017). However, domestic tourism in the backpacking scenes discussed in this book is incredibly rare. Indeed, the TAT has also sought to reposition Thailand less as a backpacking haven for young people seeking adventure on a shoestring budget and now actively recruits "high-quality" international tourists who generate larger revenues (Sakwit 2020). These tourists have more disposable income and have displaced other types of travelers and infrastructure; what used to be economical and well-trod backpacking routes are more challenging to find, and privately owned accommodations and transportation options are being replaced with new ventures owned by wealthy elite and multinational corporations.

Efforts to diversify tourism and curate Thailand for international markets have not completely disrupted eroticized representations, as new ventures often reestablish a link between Thailand and intimate bodily care; the economy still relies heavily on the aesthetic, bodily, and emotional resources of Thai women (Sunanta 2014; Van Esterik 2000). Moreover, it is not only images but also affects that are fundamental agents shaping Thailand. Affect materializes the imaginaries of tourists who comment on how the country feels sexually charged and draw on cultural idioms to describe how Thailand is more laid back (*sabai sabai*) than their home country with a no worries (*mai pen rai*) attitude, notions that reverberate with perceptions of sexual tolerance and adventure. While research has focused extensively on how this eroticization has affected Thai women, what is less discussed is how Thai men are also enmeshed in struggles over representation, capital, and sexuality in tourist markets.

Thailand is often considered to be brimming with sexual appeal for male tourists, but the islands in particular are sexual playgrounds for female tourists. Romantic and sexual intimacies—both long and short term—are common in the fire dance scene, and most dancers have had relationships with tourists. Fire dancers must carefully navigate these intimacies, because the sense of eroticism that surrounds the scene, alongside the heavy partying, drinking, and drug use at the beach parties, generates social narratives that position fire dancers as deviant beach boys who are only after easy money, partying, and access to *farang* tourists. As such, fire art is not considered to be an acceptable form of labor, and it does not conform to the type of image the Thai state wants to project; idealized presentations of Thai musical culture highlighting classical and folk music dominate tourist marketing. Fire dancers are positioned awkwardly in notions of Thainess, and curated images of the country do not feature fire art. Fire dance performances are a contradiction in that they are strikingly in and out of place; they are a ubiquitous part of the tourism industry and yet erased from Thai national imaginaries and tourism marketing.

While fire dancers mostly perform at beachside venues frequented by young backpackers, they touch on other markets. Some dancers perform for and interact with the world's wealthiest at luxury resorts and private villas, others might provide shows at weddings, and beach performances may also have organized tour groups in the audience or families who stop by as they wander back to their hotels after dinner. Because of the diversity of international tourists on the islands, dancers are transnational figures skilled at conversing with people from all over the world and adaptable to the changing patterns of tourism. In 2019, for instance, I noticed that dancers had been learning Mandarin to interact with the waves of Chinese tourists who had been coming to the islands. The dancers are highly cosmopolitan, often speak multiple languages, and participate in a range of global popular cultures, and many have traveled abroad. Yet dancers are also tied to their lives, values, and families in rural home villages in Thailand and Myanmar, which crosscut their global positionalities on the beaches. To their families, some are considered highly successful and are praised for their ability to send home money to their villages and take care of their parents and/ or wives and children; others are considered failures for pursuing what is often deemed an unacceptable job. To the bar owners who hire them, fire dancers are foremost an economic boost to their business and are easily replaceable with the large influx of fire dancers from Myanmar. At their nightly performances, fire dancers are often interpolated as sexualized figures by tourists, a perception that is heightened because of their affective labor in the industry and the desires and histories that shape imaginaries of Thailand.

Affect, Labor, and Mess

Affect is fundamental to how fire dancers understand and create their worlds—it is a platform for the creation and management of identities, and fire dancers hone their craft of relating to tourists and to each other through emotions and intensities. The use of these two words—emotions and intensities—to describe affect may give some readers pause; one describes a conscious feeling, while the other refers to something more akin to an unconscious energetic force. Affect theories often make distinctions between these perspectives, and the affective turn has ushered in two separate approaches: new materialism and cultural affect theory. New materialist affect theories build off the philosophies of Baruch Spinoza and consider affect as preconscious intensities that affect a body's capacity to act. Affect is thought of as different from conscious, subject-centered emotions and is understood as sets of forces that relationally and dynamically produce bodies and worlds, conceptions that challenge social constructivist perspectives (Barad 2007; T. Brennan 2004; Clough 2008; Deleuze and Guattari 1983, 1987; Gregg and Seigworth 2010; Manning 2007; Massumi 2002). Cultural affect theory, built from the work of feminist and queer scholars, argues for the importance of studying named and conscious affective underpinnings that connect bodies and social worlds (Ahmed 2004; Berlant 2011; Cvetkovich 2003; Kosofsky Sedgwick 2002 Love 2009; Muñoz 2006).

The difference between these two perspectives surrounds the ontology of affect: as either preconscious intensities circulating among bodies, objects, and spaces or conscious forms of emotionality that are brought into the realm of cognition and language. However, affective ontologies must be understood first and foremost as culturally and socially contingent phenomena. In the fire dance scene, it is necessary to obscure the line between affect and emotion in order to attend to "the culturally variable and locally articulated ways that feelings and desires escape the body and meet, or affect, each other" (Cassaniti 2015a, 140). The affective worlds of fire dancers are not easily parsed. Fire dancers articulate and experience the affective realm as energy, power, vibes, and specific emotions that can be experienced individually but that also circulate among bodies, spaces, and beings to generate social effects.

Anthropologists of emotion, and particularly those working in Southeast Asia, have advocated for the importance of considering emotions as constituted through social and cultural worlds (Cassaniti 2015a, 2015b; Geertz 1973; Lewis 1990; Boellstorff and Lindquist 2004; Keeler 1983; Lutz and White 1986; Rosaldo 1980, 1984; Rosaldo 1989). Many foundational studies in Southeast Asia have been conducted in contexts with linguistic and ethnic homogeneity (Boellstorff and Lindquist 2004). Tourist contexts present complex webs of sociocultural, political, religious, and linguistic influences. In such spaces, affective experiences are woven through transnational, regional, and local systems of meaning; on the tourist islands, affective intensities are potentially felt, named, and experienced differently among social actors in the same space. This presents unique challenges for research that forefronts affect.

Thinking about affect through a new materialist lens—as unnamed dynamic intensities—provides a valuable starting point, particularly in the worlds of fire dancers, which are influenced by Southeast Asian cultural orientations and animist ontologies that have long considered the transference of forces—such as power and emotion—among people, spirits, objects, and landscapes (Allerton 2009; Århem 2016; Errington 1989; Guillou 2017; Sprenger 2016). Social relations are modeled on such intersubjective and relational understandings of emotionality; getting angry in public, for example, is considered reckless behavior, as it not only disturbs the smoothness of social interactions but also disrupts the feelings of others. Social hierarchies, in turn, are felt through the notion of *kreng jai*, which conveys how one should consider others' feelings and show deference when in the presence of those with power. Affect destabilizes notions of bounded core selves; energies circulate and permeate spaces and bodies. This is crucial when considering identities in Theravada Buddhist contexts like Thailand and Myanmar, where notions of the self are understood through the lens of impermanence (*anicca*). Fire dancers view identity as dynamic sets of possibilities influenced by affect rather than as fixed categories. These understandings resonate with new materialist theories, and yet these forces can also be named and are very much conscious (Cassaniti 2015a). Here, I employ "affect" to describe intersubjective emotional phenomena that are mediated through bodies, objects, and spaces. These felt intensities might be named or unnamed, consciously known or lying below the surface of cognition as they are cultivated, exchanged, and expressed. Ultimately, affect is a bodily experience; it is sensed through everyday practices and ushered forth through performance each evening by fire dancers.

Affect is a key component of fire dance labor—it is moved and exchanged among bodies to create feelings on the beaches, and it is generated and managed by dancers through performance, conversation, and interactions. The affective labor of fire dance extends beyond performances and entertainment on the beaches; fire dancers invoke particular energies to create distinctions between morality and immorality through a process Julia Cassaniti refers to as the "moralization of emotion" (2014, 281). Discourses of morality in Thailand are largely shaped by Theravada Buddhism and are pervasive in official law as well as in personal relationships. The significance of morality cannot be understated as it relates to the laws of karma (*kam*) and the underlying logic that "all (moral) actions have (moral) consequences" (Stonington 2020, 762). One gains merit (*bun*) through moral actions. The more merit one has, the better one's rebirth and positioning in the cosmological hierarchy. Immoral behaviors can result in penalties (*bab*) against one's merit. While most Thais are not experts at Buddhist philosophy or scripture, these ideals permeate social life in Thailand and Myanmar, as both countries are close to 90 percent Theravada Buddhist.

Dancers use affect as a mechanism of creating moral selves as they grapple with their immersion in neoliberal capitalism and attempt to shift social perceptions of fire dancers from immoral beach boys to artists. Affects are valuable currency in this emotional economy. They demonstrate one's motivations and intensions to others, and they are fundamental in forging relationships and defining the boundaries of belonging in the fire dance scene. Affective moralities are felt among bodies, and they are incorporated into fire dance aesthetics. Particular motivations and desires are thought to break through and appear on the surface through gestures and movement aesthetics that signal intentions to others. How someone dances, learns to dance, and even observes or participates in dance is considered analogous with moralities.

This affective production of morality can, however, contradict the lived realities and desires of dancers who are seduced by the pleasures and opportunities afforded in tourism contexts. A common moral clash surrounds idealized notions of artistry as being removed from economic exchange. Money is considered to be a corrupting worldly attachment in Theravada Buddhist teachings. The tempering of money's force is particularly pronounced in musical relationships where morality is cultivated through reciprocity among performers and audiences (Mitchell 2011; Tausig 2014). Social relations in Thailand are permeated with, and maintained through, similar logics of exchange in kin economies; the principles of kin economies are "generally guided not by extracting and accumulating profit . . . but by the need to define, maintain, or elaborate relationships" (Wilson 2004, 12). These economies link to social and spiritual morals and relationships, and thus they are focused on creating affective ties. These systems are considered antithetical to capitalist logics and economies, although they are very much intertwined, particularly in the worlds of fire dancers.

This book pays particular attention to these dissonances and considers how incommensurable affects collide in moments of "friction" and create new possibilities, relations, and worlds (Tsing 2005). These forms of worlding are a significant part of the stories told here. To fully illuminate the generative potentials of tourist economies requires a different way of looking at the industry. In many ways, tourism perpetuates colonial capitalist violence as it intersects with race, ethnicity, nation, gender, class, and sexuality. Yet tourism industries are not solely sites of destruction, because within them a multitude of world-making projects emerge. The connections and encounters at a tourist site are an assemblage that "don't just gather lifeways; they make them" (Tsing 2015, 23). Tourist labor is simultaneously violent and life affirming and filled with both hope and despair.

I am inspired by Eve Kosofsky Sedgwick's call for reparative approaches that consider lives and experiences beyond the "hermeneutics of suspicion" that underpin critical inquiry.[7] By resisting tendencies to expose forms of oppression that ultimately confirm what is already known, a reparative approach follows lines of affect through everyday knowledge and experiences which can lead to unanticipated discoveries and surprises (2003, 124–50). How do people make lives hopeful, joyful, and livable in tourist contexts? What affective mechanisms sustain communities of laborers in the face of oppressive forces? What transformative possibilities might sites of tourist capitalism generate? Answering these questions illuminates experiences of touristic labor and contexts that are not easily categorized or resolved—tourism and the affects it generates are messy.

While "mess" is often negatively associated with disorder, this book engages with Martin Manalansan IV's conception of mess as a queer logic that values disarrangement and dissonance, resisting the tidiness, order, and categorization of the normative (2018). While recognizing how fire dancers are positioned as deviant subjects in transnational economies of race, gender, and desire, queerness is invoked here beyond identitarian frameworks. Logics of queerness help to elaborate how peripheral social actors employ everyday practices to create new possibilities and maneuver within a range of normative regimes (Manalansan IV 2015). For fire dancers, this means oscillating between fulfilling desires that arise from their participation in tourist markets and wanting to be seen as moral artists as defined by their own values, as well as normative models of Thainess; those aims facilitate both radical resistance to and complicity in neoliberal capitalism, colonial erotics, and national politics.

Affect provides a path to trace these entanglements through the dancing body and the lives of dancers: affect bonds, it divides, and sometimes it spins off in uncontrollable ways, creating new opportunities. The affective work that surrounds fire dancers' reimagining of themselves and their communities can be simultaneously hopeful and destructive: it produces avenues of solidarity and intimacy that would otherwise be impossible and unimaginable outside of tourism; and it links into systems of domination and colonialism. The dancing body is the platform where such negotiations ensue as dancers confront the intertwining of fire art with neoliberal capitalism and national and transnational regimes of race, ethnicity, class, gender, and sexuality.

Methodological Approach

The ethnographic research for this book was conducted in 2015, 2016, and 2019, with more contextual data drawn from my experience living in Thailand from 2010 to 2013. The research was multisited and centered primarily on two tourist islands, Koh Samui and Koh Phi Phi, although I also conducted interviews and participant observation with fire dancers in Bangkok, on Koh Phangan, and on Koh Lanta. There is a very large fire dance scene on Koh Tao, although I intentionally avoided going there and was advised not to pursue research on the island, for good reason. Koh Tao has been mired in controversy since the murder of two British tourists for which two Burmese laborers—Zaw Lin and Win Zaw Htun—were charged and given the death penalty which has been subsequently commuted to life in prison. As has been widely reported, the investigation had significant flaws, gaining international attention for suspicions that the police covered up for a more likely suspect. Following this case, there were other mysterious deaths and controversies. The *Koh Samui Times* published a piece calling Koh Tao "Death Island," which resulted in authorities filing a defamation lawsuit against the English-language newspaper. This case and subsequent murders damaged Thailand's international image and brought to light not only the dangers of traveling there but also dark secrets about police corruption and the harsh treatment of Burmese laborers. At the time of fieldwork, this was still a very sensitive topic, and any person asking questions and interviewing Burmese workers was met with distrust.

The abhorrent treatment of undocumented laborers in Thailand is the focus of human rights activism in the country, work that was dangerous under the strict policies of the ruling military government at the time of fieldwork. It was risky at times to work directly with Burmese dancers, although I spent time with them informally. The two Burmese dancers I did interview and share time with on Koh Samui in 2016 were students of a Thai dancer. I was able to return in 2019 to spend time with a team of Burmese dancers in a safe place, which provided an opportunity to fully immerse myself in their worlds. On Koh Phi Phi, I also spent time with Burmese dancers informally after the shows and during the beach parties, but I was warned to be careful about what I wrote from these encounters. Many of the islands are economically and politically controlled by powerful mafia families, and tourists or expats who cause trouble sometimes do not make it back to the mainland. These deaths are often treated as suicides and never fully investigated. Indeed, even working with Burmese dancers on some islands proved sensitive, and I was warned about being careful with my publications if I ever wanted to return to the islands. While the focus of this ethnography is on Thai dancers in what is referred to as the first and second generations, the third generation of Burmese dancers are ever present, and their experiences are interwoven into the discussions and themes explored here.

I conducted over thirty-five formal interviews and had many more informal conversations, as dancers preferred to tell me about their lives at moments they felt were appropriate; this often happened spontaneously while we were on a *motocy* (motorcycle), while we were practicing a new fire art move, or when we were eating together. Interviews happened in the midst of doing something else, and I came to build knowledge with fire dancers as part of daily interactions. This theoretical orientation developed organically during fieldwork through an approach rooted in grounded theory that builds theoretical frameworks from the data collected (Charmaz 2006); theory for this research emerged from patterns—linguistic, affective, and embodied—that came about through interacting with fire dancers. In analyzing these data during and after fieldwork, I examined how and where particular patterns emerged and looked at them alongside wider sociocultural codes and my own experiences, oftentimes with fire dancers who contributed to finding themes.

The choice to do multisited research emerged through a methodological approach that followed fire dancing and fire dancers. Fire dancing is a mobile scene, and most dancers perform all over the islands and travel back and forth to Bangkok or their home villages frequently, although those from Myanmar are not able to do so regularly because of their undocumented status. Fire dancers all over Thailand move in this way and are interconnected; I quickly learned that the dancers on Koh Phi Phi knew the dancers I was working with in Bangkok and on Koh Samui in the Gulf of Thailand. I moved like them and traveled back and forth between the islands, the mainland, and Bangkok multiple times on buses, boats, trains, and planes. My methodological approach is strongly rooted in embodying the experiences of particular ways of life through movement practices (Kisliuk 1998; Sklar 2001). Thus, I developed a sense of the everyday rhythms of fire dancers and tourists who move around the country on these same routes.

I also learned and practiced flow art, namely, studying *poi* spinning and hula hoop. Given the high degree of importance dancers place on determining peoples' relative morality based on their movements and affects, I not only developed a bodily knowledge through this approach but also gained trust by getting into rhythmic and affective affinities with dancers, which allowed me to become attuned to the indirect communicative powers of affect. This sometimes entailed traveling all over the country, sitting for hours and napping, or sharing food and cleaning up. At other times, it meant helping to set up for performances, riding around islands on *motocy* collecting equipment and kerosene, jamming on instruments at Thai reggae bars, and even getting up on stage for tourists with fire whirling around my body. My position as a young white woman from Canada impacted how much I was privy to in a largely male scene. Given the gendered dynamics of fire dance and the Thai social mores concerning feminine respectability, I found it most appropriate to learn fire dance as a student. This enriched my perspective and it also provided a reason for continuous interaction with fire dancers, although tensions remained, which I discuss most prominently in chapter 7. Because sexual relationships between fire dancers and tourists happen frequently, my presence with dancers aroused suspicion and sometimes anger—not from fire dancers, but from others who were involved in their worlds.

As a researcher affiliated with an elite Thai university and having a higher socioeconomic status, at times I held a powerful position on the beaches. As will be demonstrated, however, power shifts and changes quickly in the fire dance scene, and sometimes I had little social power and had to follow the demands of those around me.

In learning flow art and moving around the islands as dancers do, I was able to gain a feel for fire dance worlds, which is a pertinent aspect of knowledge in a country where many things are left unsaid or simply cannot be said. One must feel one's way through the sociopolitical landscape in Thailand. Because of the country's strict lèse majesté laws, saying anything even remotely critical about the royal family is a crime punishable by fifteen years in prison for each offense. Trials are typically not public, because even repeating what has been said is an offense. After the ruling junta took power through a coup in 2014, there was an increase in these charges. At the time of fieldwork, the law was being widely interpreted so that almost any form of protest or criticism could be manipulated in this way. As another method to silence dissent, the military banned the use of certain words at academic conferences and developed "attitude adjustment" camps where people were taken if they did not comply. Thais have often found other ways to discuss political life, through coded language and material culture (Tausig and Haberkorn 2012), sounds (Tausig 2019), and gestures (Herzfeld 2009). Other things are left unsaid but still very much known, and there were many times during fieldwork where I felt that I and the people around me wanted to discuss an issue but were too afraid. You must discern how the people around you feel before speaking about anything political in Thailand, and it can take years to build trust. Overall, however, I found this concern with speech and sociopolitical tensions much more pronounced during fieldwork than when I lived in Thailand prior to the military takeover in 2014.

Although I studied Thai, I am not a fluent speaker, and dancers preferred to speak with me in English. Sometimes a dancer would use a Thai word in an interview or conversation to be precise, and some questions I framed in Thai, but most of our interactions happened in English. Because of the intercultural nature of fire art, there are Thai, French, Russian, Japanese, American, and Burmese artists who sometimes work together, and the language used among all is typically English. Because of this, I often had to go back to dancers and ask specifically in Thai what they had meant, and we worked together in the field and over social media to find the precise words and terminology. In this way, it is not so much that our interactions were in one particular language; rather, we actively *did* language together, discussing and choosing the correct Thai or English phrase for a particular moment or experience.

The use of the terms "tourists" and "locals" or "laborers" presents incomplete and generalized labels for vast intergroup differences. This is important to recognize in the tourism industry in Thailand, where there are local laborers from different regions, cities, provinces, and countries who all work on the beaches. In turn, Thailand supports many different types of tourists: young backpackers on a budget who sometimes also work at beach bars for room and board, English teachers employed in Thailand and throughout Asia, organized tour groups from China and Russia, families from a wide variety of countries, wealthy professionals, digital nomads, and domestic tourists. While any categorization will gloss these intricacies, for the sake of clarity I use the term "tourists" to describe international vacationers traveling for leisure. When speaking about Thai people who live on the islands, I use "inhabitants" to reflect the cultural knowledge that they have developed through their immersion in this world, although they may not necessarily be considered locals (Ingold 2011). All dancers' names are pseudonyms based on Thai and/or Burmese nicknames that are used in day-to-day conversations.

Among fire dancers, there are many terms used to describe their art, and even the same people would articulate their practice differently at different times. It is variously called fire dancing, fire art, fire spinning, fire juggling, and playing fire. I have, in this case, chosen the word "dance" because this is a term almost all people used at one point or another, although in interviews and for stylistic purposes I also employ other descriptors. As will be demonstrated, however, different descriptors can be used to invoke notions of social belonging and social difference. Thus, in thinking about dance, I am not so much concerned with the meanings attached to the word but rather view dance as performative movement that both reflects and creates relationships—political, social, cosmological—through moments of social exchange (Henry, Magowan, and Murray 2000). Moreover, in considering the intersections of dance and tourism, I examine dance as a vital form of agency that mediates local and global processes, subjectivities, and the mobility of people and capital (Alexeyeff 2009).

Chapter Outline

Chapter 1, "Transforming Fire Dance Surfaces," examines the transformations that fire dancers undergo through their labor and the desires of tourists. It demonstrates how an eroticized neoliberal identity supports fire dancers to gain income. I draw on interviews with *farang* women to examine how dancers become erotic figures through racialized colonial affects and imaginaries and how fire dancers navigate the increased social and economic capital such imaginaries can provide. I feature the perspectives of dancers on how dancing has provided opportunities to reimagine their bodies and positionalities. These transformations, however, must be carefully managed vis-à-vis an eroticization that can bring new opportunities but also increased stigma.

Chapter 2, "The Energy of Artists," explores fire dance as a form of affective labor over multiple beach sites. It elaborates what fire dancers describe as energies (*phalang*) that are generated through their corporeal work and that move among tourists to make them feel particular ways. In turn, it discusses how these energies induce feelings of masculine power for Thai and Burmese dancers that must be carefully managed in contexts of tourism. I build on theories of affective labor and the intersections of sexuality and tourism to offer new understandings of how fire dancers' labor involves becoming corporeal conduits of energies. Focus is placed on examining how dancers understand the movement of energetic material and how it is controlled to elicit a particular affective atmosphere.

Chapter 3, "Feeling Art and the Labor of Sharing," draws on research conducted with one particular lineage of fire dancers on the island of Koh Samui and discusses how fire dancers confront the changes in the fire dance scene as it shifted from a participatory communal practice in the 1990s to a performance genre situated within market capitalism. I highlight how anxieties about economic survival are projected onto the new generation of Burmese dancers who have recently arrived in Thailand. I look specifically at one fire dance team—composed of both Thai and Burmese dancers—that finds avenues to challenge such issues. The team is led by a master Thai dancer who created it as a way to contest the ethnonational and market tensions, and a system of exchange called sharing (*baeng pan*) operates among both Thai and Burmese dancers in an attempt to forge a hopeful economic existence for all dancers.

Chapter 4, "The Affinitive Labor of Freedom," centers the perspectives of Burmese dancers and examines how they reimagine the deviant subjectivities that get ascribed to them by Thai fire dancers. I examine how Burmese dancers renegotiate such positions alongside idealized masculinities in Myanmar and how they create affective moral regimes on their own terms in search of what they define as freedom. The chapter details the stories and particular circumstances of young Burmese men and how their labor on the beaches is a locus for the formation of affective bonds of belonging in Thailand.

Chapter 5, "The Everyday Comfort of Practice," explores the ordinary affects of island life for Som, a dancer on Koh Samui. Focusing on his daily pattern of practicing on the tourist beaches, this chapter centers affects of comfort and contentment. I highlight how a *sabai sabai ethos*—an iconic Thai idiom that references contentment—operates in Som's life and how hope and a sense of precarity influence his pursuits and dreams of the extraordinary.

Chapter 6, "Striving on Koh Phi Phi," is situated on the small tourist island of Koh Phi Phi and discusses the quiet destruction of ecosystems, economies, and livelihoods after the 2004 Indian Ocean tsunami. I center the insights and affective contestations of one fire dancer, Nam. I elaborate the ways in which he lives hopefully amid the violence of tourism and neoliberal capitalist expansion on Koh Phi Phi. His striving toward his goal (*chut mung mai*) elaborates an affective politics that connects Nam to "secret histories" of people who strive with him.

Chapter 7, "Fire Dance Femininities," investigates the disappearance of female Thai fire dancers over the last ten years and features the perspectives of the last remaining female fire dancers in the country. The chapter highlights the ways in which gender and sexuality operate in relation to spatiotemporal contexts (*kalatesa*). It explores the fluidity of gendered expression and how certain spaces and times have allowed female fire dancers to contest colonial and nationalist representations of Thai femininity but how other contexts have limited their abilities for such bodily engagements. This chapter also features autoethnographic writing that discusses my own complex engagements in this scene—as a white woman learning to fire dance among men—and the reasons why gender, sexuality, and race were animated in some spatiotemporal contexts and not others.

There are possibilities and limitations generated in contexts of tourism. Tourism is a mess of an industry in which affects, moralities, neoliberal capitalist labor, and community provide both hopeful and violent possibilities. Fire dancing is an activity that invites contemplation on the hopes and pleasures of tourist industries as well as the destruction and despair those industries bring. This book centers the concepts fire dancers embody to mediate tourism and find avenues to "feel together," as one fire dancer describes it, and highlights the potentials for applying such frameworks toward wider political ends.

TRANSFORMING FIRE DANCE SURFACES

I have moments in my life that are very cool for me, like when everything is connecting. So many things changed my mind, like meeting
different people and connecting. And this is some black magic, you
know. Spirits—I never believed before, but I believe now. Because they
show me. I feel I've changed a lot in my life. Now things are going well.
Ya, it's not only you in the world. Many people are watching you that
you can't see. There are spirits on another level. I'm very lucky. I've
met a lot of rich people and they want to try to be like me now! Haha!

—Som

I had many philosophical conversations with Som, a fire dancer who grew up in
a village in the Northern Thai province of Uttaradit. He often joked with me
about how many times I would hear the village-to-beach story of fire dancers as
I did my research. He explained early on during fieldwork that "all the people
who have this job were sad when they were young," and this was the case for
Som, who was aware of the somewhat unimaginable transformations that can
happen through being involved in the tourism industry. He reflected on his
younger years spent picking coconuts to support his family and how his dirty
brown school uniform—which had been worn down over the years from its original black—was a mark on his body that cast him as the poorest among other
village children. Som, through a series of unanticipated meetings, travel, and
connections, ended up working at a shop in the tourist district of Bangkok and
later became a fire dancer. For Som, there was a magical thrust that helped forge
these life paths and opportunities. At the time of fieldwork, he was one of the
most highly paid dancers in the country, performing solely at large beach events
that ushered in vast shifts in social and economic power in Som's life. As he states
above, now rich people want to be like him.

The village-to-beach story among fire dancers is ubiquitous, and almost all
dancers I consulted had moved to a tourist area and saw their lives dramatically
change as new economic and social possibilities emerged from the encounters,
friendships, and opportunities on the beaches. These changes shift fire dancers'
identities, which are individually crafted and influenced by the local, global, and

regional politics that intersect in tourist sites. Identity is an unstable concept in Theravada Buddhist contexts such as Thailand where ideologies of impermanence (*anicca*) and possibilities to move through cosmic hierarchies based on actions (*karma*) generate a sense of self that is a fluid and relational (High 2014; Käng 2014; Morris 1994; Van Esterik 2000). Fire dancers' experiences echo logics of dynamism and creative shapeshifting in an industry that provides opportunities to make oneself anew. Yet such potentials are also countered by social, political, and economic forces that attempt to constrain malleability and define dancers, often as sexualized and marginalized figures. This push and pull requires a pliable understanding of identity as sets of circumstances that *happen* in particular times and spaces—that is, as events that people shape and negotiate (Saldanha 2007).

Penny Van Esterik's (2000) theorization of gender in Thailand elaborates the eventfulness of identity through the notion of a "gendered surface" that can change depending on contexts of time and place (*kalatesa*).[1] One's surface can be composed of styles of speech, tone, accents, and dress as well bodily comportment and gesture. There are great possibilities for transformation, but it is knowledge of context that is crucial for shaping surfaces appropriately. How people dress, act, speak, and behave can be vastly different depending on the situation, who is present, and what types of social power or respect (*barami*) they should be afforded. The logic of surfaces can be extended beyond gender to consider how people shape themselves, how they are shaped by others, and how class, race, sexuality, and ethnicity are changing phenomena in the worlds of fire dancers.

Becoming Beach Boys

During my first week on Koh Phi Phi, I took the ferry back to Krabi to go to the Department of National Parks and get permission to carry out research in Hat Hapharat Thara-Mu Koh Phi Phi National Park. I arrived and met the head of that area. He had some familiarity with my project, since I had previously sent documents from the National Research Council of Thailand. I sat across from him, and he seemed quite interested in my research. I was slightly taken aback, as most Thais responded to the project with ambivalence and sometimes even embarrassment and confusion at why someone would focus on a practice that is not valued in Thailand or even viewed as art. About two minutes into the conversation with the official, his true interest in my project revealed itself. He asked if we might work together and proposed that instead of researching fire dance, we try to change the practice. He wanted fire dancing to stop, he explained, because it was bad for the environment and "dirty."

Indeed, environmental destruction in the national park was top of mind because the increasing intensity of tourism was destroying the ecosystem; the iconic Maya Bay from the movie *The Beach* had recently been closed to tourists so that the coral could recover. I was, however, perplexed at how fire dancers—who are so incredibly careful with their equipment and accelerants—were to blame for disrupting the ecosystem; on the islands there is an endless stream of boats carrying tourists who leave beaches filled with garbage, destroy coral and marine life through scuba diving, and demand the continued building of tourist infrastructure; yet it was the fire dancers, in his mind, who were dirty. I skirted around a commitment to him, knowing that any partnership I had with a government official would end my relationships with fire dancers. Luckily, he approved my research. His proposal must have faded from his mind, as I never heard of it again. However, this narrative about fire dancers was a pervasive one.

For many Thais, fire dancers are a source of shame and often considered deviant beach boys who contaminate the image of the country. The term "beach boy" invokes a sense of entrepreneurial deviancy with an underlying eroticism: a male beach laborer from a poor background who works on the tourist beaches to develop relations with tourists, sometimes for income or other opportunities. Because of the nature of their labor, which involves connecting with tourists, fire dancers navigate widely circulating beliefs that they are involved in the art form only so that they can have access to, and intimacies with, tourists. It is not uncommon to hear fire dancers discussed as dangerous and uneducated young men who are in search of quick money and who do drugs, drink too much, and prey on tourist women. This framing is also a product of fire dancers' village-to-beach pathways, described by Som at the beginning of this chapter.

In her research with migrant Thai male laborers on the beaches in Koh Phagnan, Linda Malam found that they were viewed by inhabitants as deviant and suspicious because of their placelessness; they were displaced from familial systems of morality that would normally shape their behavior. However, the respect these workers lacked in the wider social space of the island was counteracted in the tourist beach bars where they performed a hypersexual and powerful heterosexual masculinity associated with toughness, womanizing, and heavy drinking—that is often referred to as *nak leng* or *chai chatri* (Malam 2008 a and b). These hegemonic Thai masculinities encapsulate idealized qualities such as being "brave, daring, risk-taking, and fair" (Sinnott 2004, 88) but also imply that a man is tough and has numerous sexual intimacies with women (Ockey 1998; Shulich 2009). In tourist spaces, enacting a *nak leng* or *chai chatri* gendered surface is a way for Thai men to assert power, particularly over *farang* men in contexts shaped by white neoliberal capitalism, and gain the attention of *farang* women. But this empowered masculinity must be carefully negotiated in different spaces; outside the beach bars, these men lack the social and economic capital to enact such gendered empowerment. As migrant laborers in the beach backpacker scene, fire dancers face similar perceptions and limitations. They must carefully craft different gendered surfaces depending on context.

Fire dancers have a significant amount of power with *farang* in the beach bars and parties where they work. While not all engage in heavy drinking, most fire dancers do socialize with tourists as part of their job and for pleasure. Their migrant routes mean that they often form communities at the bars with tourists, other laborers, and expats. Dancers can appear as the most influential and important people during the beach parties, even though they might hold very little social and economic power at bars, which are often owned by Thai elite; this is especially true for Burmese dancers who rely on the good nature of their employers to allow them to continue to live and work in the country. However, the beach bars offer a particular time and space for *nak leng* masculine surfaces to appear; tourists often comment on how fire dancers are flirtatious and sexy, even though fire dancers may not intend this. As fire dancers shape themselves as powerful young men, in ways not afforded to them outside of the bars, particular affects and imaginaries also shape their surfaces offering both transformative opportunities and increased precarity and stigmatization.

That fire dancers invoke an erotic draw for *farang* women is widely discussed among touristic laborers, expats, and tourists. Naomi, a white woman originally from the United States, came to Thailand on vacation and ended up moving to the small island of Koh Lanta to marry a fire dancer. She explained when she first saw her husband:

> The first time I ever saw Tan he was fire dancing. I thought he was the sexiest man I'd ever seen. But I didn't notice him earlier in the day, in the bar, until he came out fire dancing. I think it's unexpected. I didn't know that Thai men were super-hot. So, when I got here, I was kind of shocked by it—like, the sexuality that they put out. They are very comfortable with themselves, with their bodies, and with what they do with tourism and with women. They are used to it. Some of them aren't new to the industry. They've been working in it since they were quite young and so they have a comfort and a confidence about them that I never really noticed in a man. Nancy [her friend] and I were talking about this in our first year here, about how they are in tune with their masculine and feminine side.

Her friend Nancy, who is originally from Israel and married to a former fire dancer, Tune, nodded in agreement and laughed: "Oh so much! And I feel like it is very obvious in the dance. The way they move their hips, the way they move their body. Not only in fire dancing, but in general, I feel like they are much more connected to their feminine side than Western men in my country." Having both lived in Thailand for over five years at the time of fieldwork, Nancy and Naomi had an astute understanding of Thai culture and the lives of fire dancers. They were critical of the sexual imaginaries that shaped dancers in this way. But also note it was an unexpected desire and sexuality that drew them to their fire-dancing husbands initially.

While fire dancers do not consider the art form to be erotic in any way, these types of sentiments were shared frequently by *farang* women. Many commented on what they felt was an unanticipated attractiveness of Thai men, often expressed through racist and orientalist notions. A conversation with one German woman who was dating a fire dancer exemplified this: "The first time I came here, I thought never I will be with Thai boy. I thought that they are small. They are skinny." These sentiments reference global hierarchies of masculinities and reverberate with the long-held positioning of Thailand as a feminized space of sexual fantasy. It's clear that the colonial tropes that have sexualized Southeast Asian women have also impacted men.

Fire dancers become erotic figures as they ignite white colonial imaginaries and tourists' desires for "radical bodily difference" (Desmond 1999, xiii). In her research on performance in Hawaiʻi's tourism industry, Jane Desmond finds that the iconic hula girl and the beach boy surfer were safely racialized; they were cast as brown bodies—not black—and were constructed as Others in ways that engaged American tourists' desires for exoticness vis-à-vis white anxieties of blackness. The brown bodies of fire dancers play on exotic imaginaries of Thailand in similar ways; they are feminized and present an exotic difference that is aesthetically safe and surprising for tourists. This tourist desire for Otherness was communicated ubiquitously by *farang* women, and many laborers joked about the weekly arrival of white Scandinavian women who would become enthralled with the brown bodies of fire dancers. Indeed, most female tourists I spoke with were not aware that most "Thai" fire dancers are from Myanmar— their bodies showcased a form of difference that was desired, regardless of where they were from.

Fire dancers relate that the goal of their performances is to attract people to the bars, keeping their attention through performance but also through conversation and general entertainment. While much of this attraction is, at its core, affective work that is discussed in chapter 2, it is also bodily work. Fire dancers are well aware of tourists' desires for bodily difference, and they carefully shape their surfaces toward dominant white Eurocentric masculine aesthetics while balancing what tourists perceive as exotic. As such, they do not typically embody dominant Thai masculine ideals. Their heavily tattooed bodies, long hair, piercings, hard bodies, and beach-style clothing of flip-flops and board shorts are just some of the surface adornments that position them outside the Thai middle class and elite.

Fire dancers tend to have darker skin from working outside. While globalized racial hierarchies and anti-Blackness play a role in shaping perceptions about skin color in Thailand, colorism in Southeast Asia is saturated with class dynamics and Asian transnational power relations. Dark skin, often referred to as black (*si dam*), is not considered attractive in Thailand. It is associated with lower socioeconomic status and rurality and is a marker of low-paid labor. Lighter skin, or whiteness (*si khao*), represents a look of wealth and pairs with notions of being well dressed, upper class, and appropriate (*riap roi*). The desire for lightness is not always, or only, a valuing of *farang* beauty ideals, particularly among men. It also emerges from desires for East Asian aesthetics brought through the Korean Wave (*hallyu*).[2] Theses hybrid "white Asian" desires feature a soft masculinity that is associated with cosmopolitanism (Kang 2017, 8). Laborers who comb the beaches during the day selling sarongs, henna tattoos, fruit, and small souvenirs are often fully wrapped from head to toe to avoid the darkening effects of the sun, a striking opposition to the bikini-clad tourists. In trying to prevent darkening skin, they urge their surfaces toward the dominant aesthetics of whiteness. Fire dancers, however, typically let their skin darken to suit the fascination of tourists.

Fire dancers have learned to embody what they believe *farang* find attractive, and this goes beyond the skin. Fire dance requires extensive physical practice to control and manipulate the toys. To make the moves aesthetically pleasing and smooth requires detailed attention to one's balance, speed, concentration, weight, and effort. But the daily practice of dance also requires bodily work to produce a particular physique. The fire dancer's body is one produced in the image of a heavily Westernized aesthetic of work, toughness, and seduction; a fire artist's body is muscled, young, hard, and brown. The dancers are often topless in performance, and they explain that as the sweat builds on their skin while dancing, it turns into a glimmering sheen when touched by the light of the fire, accentuating their physique. Dancing topless is as much about safety and comfort from the intense heat, as one would not want a fire dancer's clothes to accidentally catch on fire, but it also showcases this bodily aesthetic.

As I was practicing with Som in front of a large mirror at a practice space he frequented, he looked at me in the mirror and related that fire dancers must be masters of the equipment and their bodies. While I initially thought he was speaking about the coordination and control that fire art requires, he was referring to bodily aesthetics: "This is an art of the body and equipment. Everything must look nice." I felt somewhat ashamed as I looked at the softer and fuller shape of my body, covered by long pants and a large t-shirt that I often wore to appear modest. Som's shirtless, hard, and chiseled body was a striking contrast to mine. It was clear, as I looked around at other dancers practicing nearby in the grass, that my body would need to be molded differently to produce the required aesthetic.

I spent many months with Som and one of his fire teams practicing at a small outdoor space that I discuss in chapter 3. Many of the dancers worked out daily with old weights that would lie about the space, and others did an extensive regime of push-ups and sit-ups every day. Py, a dancer from Myiek, Myanmar, worked out much more than the others when I first arrived. He had been back home for many months visiting his son, and his fire dance body was not as hard and defined as it had been previously, he related. I asked him about his dedicated workout routine, and he responded candidly, "Because when I do the fire show, we take off our clothes and many customers want to look at our bodies and how they move." Over the months, his soft belly transformed into chiseled abs. This aesthetic, which privileges muscles, hardness, and little fat, does not conform to the hegemonic soft Thai masculinity that is associated with higher economic status. This is a surface intentionally crafted for *farang*, and the fire dancer body becomes erotic in this way. For fire dancers, however, these surfaces must be negotiated carefully, as they can offer new social and economic possibilities but also draw increased stigma.

The eroticization that surrounds the fire dance industry presents, at times, a source of power among laborers, for instance by offering the potential for transnational friendships and intimate liaisons with tourists. *Farang* women are considered beautiful in Thailand for their white skin and Caucasian facial features. In turn, they engage desires for social and economic mobility and can reposition fire dancers as cosmopolitan or modern (*than samai*) if they are dating them. Many dancers leave the islands to move to new countries with tourists who have become intimate partners. Just as the village-to-beach journey becomes a ubiquitous migration story for dancers, so too does the island-abroad migration pattern for those looking to leave the scene.

Yet, while *farang* can be a site of admiration, they are also loathed, and fire dancers must navigate the opportunities *farang* bring with how they can reinvoke beach boy surfaces. While Thailand has been imbued with colonial sexualized fantasies, *farang* have also been sexualized and considered as sex crazed from the Thai perspective (Jackson and Cook 1999, 19). There is an ambivalence for *farang* who are at once admired and yet also considered to be morally suspect and boisterous Others not able to follow social rules. Thais often comment on how *farang* smell bad (*men*), a sensorial social judgment that comments on an unclean personhood that can affect others in close proximity. In the context of the tourism industry, *farang* do not often have knowledge of *kalatesa*—that is, how to contextually shape a gendered surface; thus, *farang* appear to dress immodestly and engage in public displays of sexuality that are considered inappropriate. While on Koh Phi Phi, a *farang* couple was videotaped engaging in public sexual activity in one of the laneways late at night. This drew national attention and intense media coverage to try to track down the tourists and have them publicly apologize for what was considered an egregious act.

These beliefs about *farang* also make their way into Thai media and politics, as seen in the wake of the 2014 murder of two tourists on Koh Chang, discussed in the introduction; General Prayuth implied that the public wearing of a bikini may be a factor in why the woman was murdered, and he stated, "Tourists think that Thailand is beautiful, safe and that they can do anything they want here. That they can put on their bikinis and go anywhere they want" (Reuters in Bangkok, 2014). While Prayuth's comments were widely condemned, the construction of *farang* female sexuality as devious, impolite, and disruptive is widespread. Relationships that emerge among fire dancers and *farang* are marked with deviancy because of the unacceptable femininity that *farang* represent.

The eroticism performed for *farang* has a clear time and space, and while it is an important part of their labor, which they sometimes enjoy, fire dancers are also deeply ambivalent about how this sexualization can reinforce narratives of them as beach boys. Som was aware of the potential and issues of fire dancers' surfaces. At our first interview, he explained, "I think that the main reason many people are doing fire art is so they can get girls easily. For me, I don't do it to get girls. I think maybe in their [tourists'] countries they don't have fire dance. So, they see brown guys with muscles and fire, and most people, you know, [motions sexual intimacy and laughs], and then go back to their home countries. For me, no. Other dancers might have a tourist girl, and they go back home, and then break up, and then another girl comes; it's the system of the bar." Som recognized his body as exotic and appealing for tourists—brown and with muscles—but he quickly moved himself away from the "system of the bar" and the notion that he was involved in the art form for intimate opportunities with tourists. While he has dated *farang* women, with some relationships lasting over a year, he was adamant that what he referred to as his playboy pursuits were something he only did in the past, and he was now critical of fire dancers who did fire art to "get girls easily." All the Thai fire dancers I spoke with were intent on distancing themselves from such eroticism and contested the beach boy surfaces ascribed to them, yet they also actively shaped themselves toward the affective imaginaries of *farang*, and all but two of the Thai dancers I worked with had dated *farang*. All dancers struggle over control of their surfaces, and they also enact agency through such pursuits, as becoming erotic not only ensures their success as performers but also can generate new pathways, perspectives, and possibilities.

Becoming White

Jes, a Burmese dancer originally from Myeik and who had been in Thailand since he was eighteen, expressed the ways in which the skin's surface can shift and change meaning in the tourism industry.

> People like difference. Me too. When I came here for the first time, I didn't like my skin because it is brown, and we want to be white. In Thailand and Burma everyone wants to be white, and they love white ladies and men. Thai ladies and Burmese ladies love white people, and you will see whitening cream when you go to 7–Eleven. So, for us, it's like, "Wow that lady is so beautiful. She's white." And white people love to be tanned haha! For us, that is crazy. We don't want to go outside if the weather is hot, but for you guys, you want to be tanned. Yes, people like difference. But now I understand it. When I was young, I used to want to be white, but now I love my skin. I love myself.

While dark skin is a marker of low status across Southeast Asia, for Jes it became a source of pride on the beaches; through the skin, and the desires that tourists invest in darkness, he became differently positioned and considered attractive in ways he would not in other spaces. As he explains, this not only changed how he was interpolated but shifted his experience of his body as he learned to love his skin in this new context.

Jes's discussion points toward the ways in which skin can be a marker of one's shifting fortunes in Southeast Asia. Theravada Buddhist beliefs in humans' abilities to move through hierarchies is transferred into the social arena; one's position at birth is not static but may change based on actions (*karma*), and the skin is a potent site where transformations are made visible (High 2014). Skin is deeply connected to class and can dynamically rewrite relations. For example, through adorning one's skin with particular jewelry, makeup, whitening creams, and coverings, one can move toward whiteness, which is associated with wealth, abundance, and beauty. Race in the fire dance scene, like gender and sexuality, is processual and is intimately linked with specific contexts.

Dark skin on the beaches becomes attractive through the desires and imaginaries of largely white tourists, while in other spaces it can imprint one's lower status on the body. Interestingly, though, fire dancers do not actively attempt to shift their skin color from black (*si dam*) to white (*si khao*) through adornments and whitening creams. Rather, they become "white"—of higher standing, socially and economically—by virtue of tourists' perceptions and their beach labor. Jes followed the path of many other fire dancers; he grew up very poor in rural Myanmar and made his way to the Thai beaches through a treacherous journey hiking and riding in the back of pickup trucks across the jungle along the Thailand-Myanmar border. While Jes makes a decent income as a fire dancer, his skin has remained dark. Rather than attempt to change it, he has come to understand his skin in new ways.

Nah, a fire dancer who had danced for over ten years, echoed these sentiments in relation to how his positioning as unattractive and poor shifted. Born in Isaan, an economically disadvantaged region in the Northeast, Nah stumbled upon tourists and Thais doing flow art in Santichaiprakarn Park in Bangkok, where he had moved during his late teens to attend a technical college. During fieldwork, he was widely known as one of the best dancers in Thailand. He lamented how, at the time when he started, he had very little money and how his lack of wealth made him "ugly" and not able to find a girlfriend. He explained how this changed as he started performing for tourists: "It's kind of a psychological thing, you know? Even if you are ugly, if you are the center of attention, you look good already. And people will feel that you are important. If you do something good, people will clap. But maybe in their [the performer's] life nothing is good at all, and they just go spin fire." Being the center of attention recast his body, although only momentarily, as it is transformed through the eyes of audience members mesmerized by his performance. Unlike Jes, Nah does not reference the exoticness of his body as a draw, but he understands this newfound attraction as an aspect of many forms of performing arts where someone is the center of attention. Through his emerging attractiveness, Nah was able to find a *farang* girlfriend. Interestingly, however, Nah points out the ways in which this new positioning can be short-lived, and he gestures to how one's attractiveness can change beyond the moment of performance where life may be "nothing good at all." However, the desiring affects of tourists that can dramatically shift one's positioning and body on the beaches can also work against fire dancers as they get cast as beach boys outside of the beach-centered tourism industry.

For Som, there was a discomfort with his emerging attractiveness, and like many other dancers, he felt that eroticism shaped his surface in ways that could lessen the respect he desired as an artist. Som knew that despite his assertion and reasons for dancing, he could be considered a beach boy preying on tourists. In our interactions, Som, like many dancers, was careful to craft a surface that highlighted his artistry and his work ethic. He further explained that although his body had a particular aesthetic that *farang* liked, it was his talent that truly affected how his socioeconomic positioning changed. As we took a break from practicing *poi* one day on the beach, we had the following conversation:

> Som: See, you are very beautiful, you are very cool, you know? People might be like, "Wow. I want to touch this girl or talk to this girl." But if I don't have talent, I can never do that, right?

AUTHOR: You think it works like that?

SOM: Ya, I have talent and that's how people think. Even older people, if you perform for them, they are like, "Wow!"

AUTHOR: Is that like respect?

SOM: Yes, because of the talent. For example, if they [points toward a group of tourists on the beach] try your *poi* and they come over and start doing tricks, you will already love them, you know? They will get you already and you will want to learn. If you see they have talent, you will respect them.

Som highlighted the way in which my skin and *farang* aesthetics positioned me on the beaches, as someone potentially untouchable or unapproachable without talent. I do not believe that Som was being flirtatious in this moment but was commenting on the same classed dynamics of skin that I speak of above, and the way whiteness and power operate in tourist economies. Som still recognized himself somewhat as a peripheral figure, regardless of his changing economic circumstances, but believed that his abilities are what changed his surface and the opportunities afforded to him.

Despite the ways in which fire dancers might come to appreciate the changes in their social and economic positionings, there are also ambivalences about these transformations. What Som and Nah express was something I commonly heard from fire dancers—a deep desire to be seen as artists and not as sexualized bodies. Yet, their labor is somewhat dependent on erotic surfaces, which opens up ruptures and creates tensions. When I first began speaking with fire dancers about this research, almost every dancer I met wanted me to know that the sexualization of fire art is solely through the eyes of *farang*, and not at all how they viewed the art form. Yet, all were aware of how surfaces and talent interacted to draw in tourists and usher in vast transformations in their lives through social and economic mobility, transnational intimate liaisons and friendships, and even new opportunities and lives abroad. In fact, fire dancers were adamant that gaining access to *farang* women was *not* why they danced nor why they started, although all recognize the prominence of tourist–fire dancer intimacies. Many spoke of how they used to be "playboys" when they first started fire dancing, a surface that was relegated to the past and an immature version of the image they now wanted to display, particularly to me as a researcher. Their surface with me was not the *nak leng* masculinity that I often saw when I watched fire dancers at work in the evenings—the masculine surface performed outside of the beach parties displayed maturity, alignment with Thai moralities, shyness, and a sense of artistry that contrasted tough, flirtatious, and erotic exteriors of the night. As a researcher, I was always left wondering: which surfaces were "real"?

Fire dancers' negotiations from context to context are in line with conceptions of the self as impermanent and in flux; these acts of shifting the surface are a valuable and essential social skill in Thailand. Their varied surfaces—those for tourists, for researchers, for communities away from the beaches, for partners—are all real, and dancers carefully mediated their context-specific metamorphoses. Perhaps some dancers are indeed focused on pursuits beyond the industry and the appeal of a having a *farang* girlfriend has waned. However, their attempts to remove these perceptions from their surfaces are also efforts to legitimize their art and labor. As they distance themselves from the behaviors they associate with the beach boy, they showcase themselves as the multifaceted individuals they are. What becomes clear is that the very narratives and constructions that can provide social and economic mobility for fire dancers on the beaches create a sense of disorder that follows them and radically rewrites these new privileges; dancers thus must work extensively to reshape their subjectivities beyond the beach-centered tourism industry and negotiate what are, at times, incommensurable hopes, desires, and aspirations against a backdrop of precarity.

Precarious Unbecomings

Getting older is one of the defining challenges of a fire dance career. To dance past thirty is a feat, and there is somewhat of a quiet, but very much known, urgency among dancers to try to learn new skills, develop new career paths, and for some, find a partner and move away to larger centers or abroad before they age out of the industry. For older dancers who have stayed in Thailand, the prosperity they once saw has greatly diminished, and they have struggled to find similar paying opportunities. Past a certain age, being able to craft the very particular bodily aesthetics becomes more difficult as bodies betray the hard work that goes into crafting a muscled surface.

Jack, a dancer on Koh Phi Phi who was in his mid-thirties, was considered old for a fire dancer, and he would joke about this with me frequently, although I also sensed that it was a real concern. Jack would run up and down the beach every day before the shows to try to craft and harden his body back to the shape it once was. When I asked Jack how long he would keep dancing, he replied, "Not sure because my body is getting old" as he patted his softening belly. Younger members on his fire dance team worried about what Jack would do for income in the next years. Pi Neung, who was among the first performers in Thailand and is credited with starting the fire dance industry in the country, was in his fifties when we met.[3] Pi Neung lamented that he could no longer make money, and he lived very humbly on the far outskirts of Bangkok making and selling fire art toys for a limited niche market. He was ambivalent that he had not found love during his years fire dancing, as many others had, as he knew that a *farang* girlfriend could help bridge transitions from the beaches to other forms of labor.

Age creeps up on fire dance bodies, changing them slowly, and is a constant reminder that fire dancing is precarious and has a time limit, particularly as the industry becomes oversaturated. The massive influx of younger Burmese dancers who are paid less by bar owners presents an ongoing threat to Thai dancers' livelihoods and surfaces; not only will the Burmese dancers perform for less money, which means they are more likely to be hired over Thai dancers, but their younger bodies mean that they are often considered the most attractive. Nam, a fire dancer on Koh Phi Phi, shared his perceptions, which are similar to those held by many of the Thai dancers I spoke with:

> Thai people work for their family, but Burmese people work for their country, and they are just working in Thailand to send money back to Burma. But they steal the Thai people's jobs and then when Thai fire artists see many Burmese people doing fire shows, they have to go to another island. Burmese guys play fire for maybe only one year and Thai guys have played for ten years and do the best shows. But now, there are too many fire shows and Thai dancers have to work at something else because they get older every day. You cannot do fire shows forever.

Thai male laborers' ability to enact an empowered surface in tourist spaces and make a decent income is seen as under threat, and new hierarchical arrangements among male laborers in the beach bars emerge as they compete in the changing market.

In addition to the sentiments expressed by Nam, fire dancers across all fieldwork sites spoke of how the Burmese fire dancers take *yaba*, a popular methamphetamine, and drink too much, that they were not interested in art, and that they only fire dance for easy access to money and women. In essence, they were not considered artists by the Thai dancers but were beach boys who gave all fire dancers a bad reputation. These perceptions reverberate with national identity politics in Thailand, which have constructed the Burmese as an aggressive enemy for centuries (Chongkittavorn 2001).

The Burmese dancers, who are often younger, threaten the livelihoods of fire dancers in the first and second generations, as well as their possibilities for social mobility and power on the beaches. Thai dancers project their fears surrounding the precarity of the industry and their own marginalization onto the surfaces of Burmese dancers. As they push the deviancy of the beach boy away from Thai surfaces and onto the younger Burmese dancers, Thai dancers shape themselves as morally superior artists, which is discussed in later chapters. Gendered surfaces are a platform where these tensions play out in a battle for meaning and control over the wider representation of fire dance, as well as access to resources in a scene where earning potential is time limited and controlled by the capitalist desires of bar owners. Because of the stigma that surrounds this form of labor, there are not as many positions readily available for those who have fire danced, which means one's years in the industry can result in increasing precarity. The fears and frustrations of Thai dancers about precarity and new migrations toward the beaches come to shape Burmese surfaces as Thai dancers attempt to re-create their own.

Fire dancers' surfaces and positionalities are made mutable through the transnational tourism industry. The racialized colonial perceptions that underpin this context are certainly worthy of intensive critique, particularly for the ways in which fire dancers become eroticized nodes in larger white neoliberal capitalist structures. However, there are also pleasure and possibility from the perspectives of fire dancers that cannot be ignored. As Jes mentions, he came to love his skin in ways that were not possible before; it was not that he transformed his skin to white (*si khao*) but rather that his skin—his surface—came to signify something different, providing a sense of admiration that he had not known previously. It was not only the physical surface aesthetics, however, that allowed for shifts in social standing and feelings about their bodies and histories as fire dancers; it was also their capacities to draw people into their worlds. As Som and Nah explain, their talent and abilities to keep people's attention—to draw them in affectively and sate their desires—set the stage for transformations. Som's invocation about the magic and spirits helping him along speaks to the unimaginability of these life changes for dancers whose serendipitous routes from villages into tourist areas have resulted in new directions and paths.

Still, however, fire dancers must carefully navigate these shifts as they desire to be seen as more than beach boys. Thus, they adjust their surfaces against a backdrop of tourists' desires and affects, while managing the precarity that lurks at the edges of a scene that abandons bodies that do not fulfill tourist imaginaries. Fire dancers' bodies mediate differentially scaled—global, local, regional—hierarchies and desires; their surfaces are marked as dirty, lower class, un-Thai and marginal, and yet these interpretations shift dramatically as they work with tourists and (re)create surfaces. Bodies that were once considered unattractive, peripheral, and poor can *become* attractive, dominant, rich, and cosmopolitan. These shifts, however, also bring with them new associations that imprint fire dancers' bodies with eroticization and exoticization that they must carefully negotiate alongside their desires to be viewed as valued artists.

THE ENERGY OF ARTISTS

It comes from yourself. Everybody has energy to come out. Everybody has different energy to come out, you know? For my own show, I like to get deep inside the music and I get people to feel the music with me. It's like an add-on. It's like when you've been to a concert and everybody is playing—like guitar, bass, all the instruments and all are perfectly together, and you feel chicken skin [goosebumps]. You know? It's the same thing. Many times, when I create a show people say, "Ah I feel chicken skin" with the music, and with the passion.

—Nah

"Energy" (*phalang*) was a word I heard often when spending time with fire dancers. How they must give it, feel it, and help others feel it formed the foundation of their skill-building and ethos as performers. Like Nah, who is quoted above, Som explained that as fire dancers, "you make the energy" and that each party has a different feeling one must work with. Nu, who danced with Som for the Full Moon, Half Moon, and Black Moon beach parties on Koh Phangan, similarly discussed this energetic aspect by relating the following about the role of fire dancers:

> First is energy. You show your energy because you are the one holding the fire. Even long ago, people who held the fire were the leaders. With fire, you feel like "Rrawwww" [roaring], like when you are going to war. You can give that energy to others, because we are energy. You know what I mean? It depends on if people understand this word "energy"— because we are energy. Like if I sit here and you sit there and if I'm moody, it might feel not good for you. You can feel me. You can feel that something is not right. If I feel good, you will feel that too. So, we give the energy and people can feel it.

Fire dancers view their roles as, most prominently, affective laborers who invite others into their feelings as they create and give energies. Not only must fire dancers ignite the affects of tourists and touch them in these sensorial ways, but they must also carefully control and conjure particular energies because of how affects impact the feelings and experiences of others.

The dancers' descriptions above speak to the porousness of bodies and the ways in which affects circulate on the beaches. The work of energy thus involves more than actively fostering intensities for tourists; dancers must carefully manage energy as it "escapes and permeates the social landscape" (Cassaniti 2015a, 135). Fire dancers' conceptions of their work with energy (*phalang*) broadens discussions of the intersections of affect and labor. Frameworks such as immaterial (Hardt and Negri 2000), emotional (Hochschild 2003), intimate (Boris and Parreñas 2010), and affective labor (Hardt 1999) highlight the production and management of emotion, intimacies, bodies, and relations. Because this work is typically gendered, scholarship has focused on women. Thailand is known "as a destination for bodily, sensual and spiritual fulfillment," and the development of the tourism industry has relied on the emotional labor of Thai women (Sunanta 2014, 8). While Thai women have become iconic representations of the fulfillment of tourist desires, Thai men also labor affectively with tourists; men are masseurs, servers, taxi drivers, sex workers, tour guides, and fire dancers providing intimate labor that often goes unrecognized.

How dancers understand their work requires expanding definitions of affective labor to account for the interembodied nature of energies. Elizabeth Wissinger argues that subjective frameworks of emotional labor do not fully encompass work that "calibrates bodily affects, often in the form of attention, excitement or interest, so that they may be bought and sold in a circulation of affects that plays an important role in post-industrial economies" (2007, 251). Fire dancers channel moods, vibes, desires, and the excitement of tourists. They use their bodies and equipment to move these affects through themselves and back out to audiences as a "conduit of affective flow" (Wissinger 2007, 263). Because certain affects can implicate fire dancers into circuits they understand as immoral, they are masters at controlling affect. Dancers perfect these affective skills and consider such abilities to be an essential mark of moral artistry.

The Energy of Artists

Som was adamant that fire dancers must practice intensely to create, manage, and share an affective connection with tourists. Som had mastered more toys and tricks than any other dancers I worked with. He typically practiced from sunrise until late into the evenings every day. Som explained that such practice creates the possibilities for affecting people emotionally, which is the mark of a serious dancer, as opposed to other dancers who he feels devalue the art form:

Som: They [nonserious dancers] just do it for fun. It's not enough. For me it's not good, you know? You shit on the equipment. Every piece of equipment has a certain charm inside.

Author: What do you mean by "charm"?

Som: Like when you really love something and when people do that thing, they get your eye. They get you and you are like, "Oh! That's amazing!" That's very hard to do because a performer needs to get your attention, you know? It takes a lot of practice. And you will see people do it not very well and be like, "What the fuck?!" It's stupid, you know? I practice very deep. This is the main thing. This is how to get the charm out of all the toys. You study deep and then when you perform you are happy because you get them [the audience], you know? Ya, I do it very deep. This is the energy of artists. It's not only, "Oh nice, clap, clap, ok let's go." This is boring. This feeling is not nice. It is very hard to get past this point. You need to be a very patient artist, practice a lot, know all the tricks and how to get people.

For Som, practicing deep sets the stage for a performer to connect and get the attention of the audience. It is one's ability to draw out and display the charm (*sane*) of each toy that makes this connection possible. This type of attraction—of "getting" the audience with charm—involves more than attracting people at a visual level; having charm is akin to an essence and appeal that touches people in a deeper, more affective way like "something that you really love," as Som expresses. A fire dancer must be able to bring out this essence from the toys and affectively attract tourists, which takes time, labor, and intensive practice with each of the toys. For Som, such practice and drawing out the special affective qualities of each different toy showcases respectability for the art form and oneself as an artist.

Som's privileging of affective connection and the energy of artists was echoed by many Thai dancers to differentiate the "real" fire dancers from those they felt were illegitimate beach boys who devalued the art form. Dancers spoke of how particular affective abilities and motivations were indicative of one's artistry, and this was often underpinned by ethnonational demarcations. Thai fire artists often employed such emotional work as a way to define themselves in opposition to dancers from Myanmar. Som stated, "There are so many Burmese people. This is not good because they steal our jobs, and they don't do a cool show. They just do it for money. It's not art, you know? Like me, I'm an artist." Pi Neung, an original fire dancer from the first generation, related, "That's why they want to do it—because they want to upgrade their life. If they know this stuff, they get more money. And they will get clever and maybe get a girlfriend or a boyfriend that maybe can bring them to Europe or America. The dancers from Myanmar will play fire for very cheap pay, you know? Because they don't really know about fire art. Like you have to make a story when you spin, go up and down with the music." As Pi Neung and Som believed, the Burmese dancers did not dance from a desire to affectively share through the art of telling a story and engaging audiences through different musical heights, or through bringing out the charm; they thought the Burmese dancers were fueled by desires for money and securing *farang* partners, which left little room for affective aspirations. Many fire dancers echoed these sentiments, which highlight how the energy of artists is linked to moral structures that are dependent on connecting with the audience.

Musician-audience relations in Thailand are underpinned by moral frameworks that privilege the formation of relationships centered in reciprocity and affective exchange. Affective relations are thought to soften the corruptive forces of monetary exchange (Mitchell 2011; Tausig 2014). When performer-audience relationships can be thought of as mutual, attachments to money are diminished and market exchange is purified; establishing emotional economies is an essential component in transforming relationships and in repositioning fire art as a valuable aesthetic form. These moralized affects liken energetic connections with tourists as purer than those situated entirely in economic exchange. Through appealing to their abilities to manipulate equipment to produce particular emotional effects, Thai fire dancers showcase the intensive skills the art form requires and reposition their labor with tourists as moral.

Fire dancers speak of how they must connect with the audience through specific techniques to ensure the morality of these relationships. For Nah, a dancer from Koh Samui, it was not only the physical practice of fire art that supported these connections but how one moved with the music to share an experience with the audience. He compared this to the melody of song and contrasted his abilities to other fire dance performances that were flat: "You cannot do just like a beat—tuk tuk tuk tuk tuk—that's not a song. Songs have a beginning, have an end, go up, go down, you understand? It needs to be like music; go straight, go up, go down and you build people's feelings like that." In building people's feelings, Nah related that he invites people to "feel the music with me." For Nah, an artist's energy is shared and he opens his body and experience of the music and movement for others to join in with him. He felt that a fire show should establish a sense of building that is a shared experience between the audience and a performer. He moves with people's feelings, providing affective heights and lulls.

Nah believed that desires for money could disrupt this energetic relationship. For instance, even though tipping is a common practice, and the most significant component of a dancer's pay on the beaches, Nah had mixed feelings about the practice and expressed that it could corrupt affective connections. He explained that tipping is not an obligation and must be carefully controlled through one's relations with the audience. About how he is teaching a group of dancers from Myanmar, he shared the following:

> I always explained to them that when you make a show, the show comes out from your feelings, and people—they can feel it. I don't recommend that they get money before the show. Customers sometimes do that, and I do not recommend that because when the dancers get money, when they feel like they got it already, then they won't feel the energy that needs to come out. Also, you cannot ask for tips, but only encourage. We look at the audience while we perform to see what tables are smiling and paying attention and then we go over to them at the end and say loudly, "Hi! Would you like a picture with us?" Everything depends on the first table you go to. If they don't tip, no other tables will. You must choose the first table carefully. We never ask for tips but must make the customers feel like they want to give money.

Nah regularly discussed his disdain for the way the new generation of Burmese dancers went table to table asking for tips and related that it can affect the energy of the show. For Nah, it was not so much the act that bothered him but the underlying intention that could accompany a performance and corrupt the affect; that is, a moral artist should be fueled by a desire to affectively connect with an audience and the audience will, in turn, feel this and want to tip. Thus, the creation of these energies can increase the social and economic power that dancers have.

Dancers expressed an awareness of, and discomfort with, these shifting positionalities, which also created the potential to develop an attachment to the self—an ego. Nah related that developing an ego was common for fire dancers and needed to be carefully controlled:

> Everyone wants to feel important and accepted. I was poor and could not get a girl. I started doing this art and everyone claps at the end. This is one of the only jobs where you get this. But this can cause an ego, especially if you only do it for women and partying. Too much ego is not good. You need to put your heart to the audience. Make them feel something. Even though we know what to do, they think fire is dangerous. We have to make them feel excited. Maybe the girls like it when a spinner has an ego, but we are not like that. And that is how you get money [tips].

Nah felt that an ego disrupted possibilities for inviting the audience to feel with him, as he says, and his technique of "putting your heart to the audience" was not possible if one has an ego. Nah related that creating this relational connection is the work of very skilled artists and that his style is less about showcasing his abilities and "more like I want you to see and feel and understand my show."

Som echoed these sentiments in one of our final interviews where he told me about the moral rules among fire dancers and explained that ego was particularly damaging to forming a connection with people. He explained that if you have an ego, "you cannot cling to anyone. You cannot go with anyone because of your ego. How are you going to perform? You need to have respect." Being an artist and generating the proper energetic connections was underpinned by these moral imperatives. To be an artist thus required self-discipline to practice the equipment to be able to draw out the charm, as Som says, but also being able to control one's own attachments to make such affectations and closeness—clinging—possible.

Interestingly, however, Nah's discussion of ego highlights an incommensurability that is prevalent throughout the fire dance scene; desires and needs for money creep into conversations about the affective moral imperatives of artistry. As Nah says above, *not* having an ego is "how you get money." While Nah is partly describing how an audience would not be comfortable and engaged with an artist who has a big ego, it is clear that a low ego has a direct financial benefit; it allows for more audience relationality and thus the potential for more tips. Som's techniques also resulted in direct economic benefits, despite his critical assessment of the new generation who he felt were motivated by monetary desires. He described how an artist moves the audience through different feeling states by layering energetic intensities on top of one another; doing this correctly determines how much the audience will tip: "I know how to get people to clap, you know? And how to feel energy. It means you have to be really cool first. To get a tip, you need to build them: show the equipment, talk first, show a little bit more and then make it hard. A lot of people they say fire dancers and fire performers are different. Performer means you know the art of everything—how to organize the show so you affect people until the end." Som often used the words "performer" and "artist" to identify those who he believed were serious and moral. Being a performer indicated a higher-level capacity to energetically build people, which had direct financial benefits.

Som discussed the connection between affect and money again with me after I watched his team's performance at a Full Moon Party on Koh Phangan:

> SOM: The energy was crazy. Good crazy. We work there and they pay for us. But another way is that we earn money by tips, so we need to really organize the show and the show needs to get more, more, more feeling to the finish. We get 4,000 to 5,000 baht every time. For me, every Full Moon Party is very challenging, you know? Because every

THE ENERGY OF ARTISTS   43

time it's young people there and it's hard to get them to tip. So, it's always a challenge and we think a lot for how to make more money.
AUTHOR: What do you do to make more money?
SOM: You need to be organized, you know? Sometimes you affect them with fire, sometimes you use the technique of the equipment, sometimes it's feeling the energy of the people and following the music.
AUTHOR: What if the energy is getting down?
SOM: We try to change it. What's really important is the finale. We need to talk about it before because when it's finished, then people give tips if they like it, you know? Normally people they come for a bit, and they are done.

Som performed for the Full Moon Parties in an open-air beach space. In such a space, as soon as people get bored, they will walk away to visit the next area of excitement. The timing and building of intensity are paramount because if the energy dips, people will leave the circle; this means there is less tipping potential when the tip bucket is passed around at the end. While audience members might wander to different beach bars across all islands, this potential is magnified during the Full Moon Party where there are multiple performances, events, and bars set up along Haad Rin Beach. These beach parties, which have upward of ten thousand people each month, are mostly for young tourists, and it takes precise planning to affectively engage them and ensure they will stay.

When I went to the Full Moon Party in August 2016, Som's team of four began by simply lighting some equipment on fire, and soon a circle of tourists began to form around them. They provided a surprise to "get them," as Som says, as one dancer took a lit torch and ran around the inside of the circle, pointing the fire close to tourists' bodies. They worked the audience, building the intensity and each trading off on particular pieces of equipment—fire injector, rope dart, *poi*, fire juggling. This led to a grand finale with LED *poi* that made designs of hearts, national flags, and words such as "love" against the dark sky, eliciting cheers from spectators. The tip bucket was passed around precisely at this moment.

For Nah, his attempts to feel *with* the audience also directly impacted earning potential. He described, like Som, how the proper layering of energy and connection is crucial and explained that the way affect is built determines how much people will drink and spend at the bar, how long they will stay, and how they will tip the dancers. His shows were structured around the rule that one cannot dance for more than thirty minutes or people will not drink, and the bar will not make money. Nah said that dancers need to make an impressive, affective show but also know when to let the energy down and become part of the background so people will stand up, mingle, and purchase alcohol. In creating energies, thus, a fire artist must also consider how much money the bar is making, as that is the ultimate reason they are hired. Not only are dancers giving particular energies to the audience, but they are simultaneously feeling them, changing their routines, and trying to assess the audience to maximize tips and income at the bar.

The energy of artists is actively manifested, and each dancer uses specific techniques that are rooted in managing one's own emotions, desires, and attachments to connect with tourists. The ability to manage these affective economies is understood as a phenomenon that delineates artists from beach boys. Generating and feeling with the audience during performances to create climactic moments, comfort, and intimacy are underpinned by moral imperatives to create relations. Even while they are entangled with economic exchange, they establish what are felt to be more enduring and important moments of affective transfer. The desire to connect with the audience is upheld as purer than dancing with an attachment to money. However, these moralized energies are also intersected by needs and desires for money. Affect is built and channeled in ways that directly financially benefit dancers and bars. And fire dancers discuss energy in specific ways to manage this incommensurability. They understand their roles in terms of giving, building, and channeling energies to the audience and making the audience feel particular qualities such as comfort, happiness, fear, and desire. Dancers, however, must not only give and feel energy with the audience but also carefully control particular affects that circulate on the beach, especially those that generate erotic effects.

Erotic Assemblages

Most fire shows begin at 8:00 p.m., as tourists are relaxing and sipping alcohol in preparation for the nightly beach parties. Dancers enter a space in the sand demarcated as a stage and provide entertainment that builds the audience toward a more club-style atmosphere that emerges after the fire dance performances have finished. This is done in very specific ways across all fire-dancing sites. Nearing the end of the performance set, audience members—typically women—are invited up on stage, and fire dancers spin fire around their bodies with *poi*. A woman will stand in front of a dancer with her body pressed close against his as he bends, twists, and manipulates the fire around their connected bodies; the optics of these interactions showcase the fire dancer as a skilled performer but also as a male protecting the female tourist from the danger of the fire around them. Audiences tend to become more boisterous during these displays, often standing up out of their chairs, moving around, and cheering.

FIGURE 2.1. Dancers leading a fire-skipping rope game with tourists after a fire show, Koh Samui.

Immediately after these interactive components, a fire dancer will walk around the crowd with a tip jar and will often wink, converse a little, and joke with tourists to create even more of a connection. These interactions are an integral part of their labor; and they are strategies for increasing the potential for tips as well as a starting point for the creation of friendships and further connections to evolve as the evening progresses. The timing of these components coincides precisely with people's intoxication levels, and it is the first instance when spatialized performer-audience boundaries begin to become more fluid. The fire dance performances culminate after the tip jar has gone around to a final interactive component when all tourists are invited to participate with dancers in fire games, such as fire rope jumping, fire limbo, and others that often result in intoxicated tourists with severe injuries.

While these interactions are very much a part of fire dancers' labor, as they are meant to encourage people to continue purchasing alcohol and have fun, they are ripe with possibilities for friendships, relationships, and sexual play. They offer insight into the porousness of boundaries between intimacies that are intentionally performed as labor in tourist contexts and those that are more emergent and that spontaneously create new relations. Boundaries between audience and dancers are permeable by virtue of the energies that are shared. Yet, when the spatial boundaries between the sand stage where dancers perform and the space where the audience sits become enmeshed, different affects emerge. These are the times when fire dancers might converse with tourists and mingle at the bar as tourists do. I've often seen fire dancers carry women under the fire limbo sticks during the games, take shots of alcohol, drink buckets, take various drugs, and dance and party with tourists. This, too, is part of the energetic building as fire dancers layer intensities, creating more and more intimacy with tourists and encouraging more intensive levels of intoxication and abandon. Fire dancers act as social lubricants and help to generate a sense of comfort, fun, and freedom that is tinged with eroticism. This plays on the linkage of travel with a sense of spontaneity, uninhibitedness, and licentiousness, and Thailand as a utopian paradise for such indulgences. What becomes clear, however, is that the affective labor of fire dancers is less about their bodily productions of erotic energies; rather, their bodies *mediate* intensities that are already being generated and passed among bodies within the space of the beach.

Because of the stigma that connects fire dancers with eroticism, it took time before dancers would speak to me about how sexuality operated in the scene. Their understandings position sexuality as one of many energetic charges on the beach that they must manage. While Nah spent months ensuring that I understood that fire artists do not do this labor to gain access to *farang* women and that they resented these associations, he opened up about the ways in which fire dance is implicated in erotic circuits: "I saw a woman get an orgasm just from watching a fire show in Koh Phangan," he said somewhat randomly one day. I was a bit taken aback, since dancers had been reluctant to speak about such a linkage, particularly with a female researcher. "Was she just sitting there?" I asked. Nah responded, "Ya, she was just sitting there with her friends, a group of girls, and she was just screaming and she had an orgasm." While Nah was somewhat perplexed at this woman's sensuous experience of fire art, he was aware of how his body became eroticized for tourists and played a role in this. But for Nah, it was not only the visual consumption of fire dancers' bodies that fueled this reaction but the way they mediated her erotic desires; it was "the energy," Nah explained.

Nah's discussion points toward a conception of the erotic as a productive desiring intensity that operates within a wider assemblage (Deleuze and Guattari 1983, 1987). This understanding was also shared by tourists who commented on how the beach was sexually charged in ways that impacted people's behaviors and interpretations of dancers. Nancy and Naomi, the *farang* wives of fire dancers discussed in chapter 1, related that it is the beach space itself, and not fire dancers, that made things feel sexual.

> NANCY: Like for me, the bar scene is . . . was very . . . um . . . something with a lot of sex, you know?

NAOMI: Sexually charged.

NANCY: Ya. Sexuality. Very charged with that.

NAOMI: Constantly sexually charged.

NANCY: And the fire show really added to that. I don't think it is the fire
dancing itself. I think it's the setting and context. Because if Tune [her
husband] would have danced here, where some of the customers are
forty years and above, families with kids, I wouldn't feel that at all.

"Here" referred to the new live music bar that Tune and she were making together. An outdoor setting with benches, small private tables, a petting zoo, and
various stages, it was a space they hoped would tame the sexual charge she associated with the beach bar that Tune had been in for years.

I asked Nancy what she meant by the sexual charge of the beach bar, and she
elaborated:

It was a bar on the beach. A lot of people came. And it wasn't a bar that I
imagined this bar to be [the one they are building]. It was a bar like des-
ignated for young people, where young people want to get drunk, young
people who want to meet cool Thai local people and hang out, *farang*
girls who want to hook up with good-looking Thai men who work in the
bar and look cool. So, in that sense. And I really didn't like it. I don't
know how I handled it for two years. I trust him completely, 100 percent,
but I just felt like when I was there, I was just torturing myself.

Nancy explained that it was "the energy of the people" that created this erotic
situation. For Nancy and Naomi, the fire dancers were simply doing their craft
in a space that is laden with sexual energy from vacationers seeking fun, risk,
sex, danger, and intimacy with locals and other tourists, understandings that
are in line with Nah's.

Considering the productiveness of tourist sexuality as intensified in these
scenes helps to intervene in discourses that position fire dancers as erotic figures that generate such sexuality; eroticism is already present and circulating
through the desires of tourists and through marketing that intertwines sexuality into tourist products (Cabezas 2009). Fire dancers are part of a larger erotic
assemblage of the beach that also involves tourists, imagery, media, music, and
capital. Fire dancers are but one component in a set of affective "technologies"
that generate the productive force of sexuality (Tan 2013). At one beach bar that
I frequented on Koh Phi Phi, a game was played after the fire shows that encouraged tourists to get naked together as the more participatory club atmosphere
got started; after the fire show, *farang* who work for room and board at that particular beach bar would come out with large signs that read "Topless ladies. Free

FIGURE 2.2.   A typical sign recruiting tourists to work in bars along Loh Dalum Bay, Koh Phi Phi.

bucket. Naked men. Free bucket." This began a process for men and women, often strangers, to get close and be daring together—while sharing potent buckets filled with alcohol—which created bonds that funneled into the club-like atmosphere in which groups of people come together on the dance floor, often merging into heterosexual couples dancing and grinding together. The beach at night was known as a place of hookups, sex in the sand, kissing strangers, grinding, and make-out sessions—what Thais would consider deviant by nature of the publicness of these sexual engagements. At the place where I stayed, the guesthouse owners had posted a sign discouraging those staying there from bringing guests back to their rooms; it was a 2,000-baht fine.

What is striking about the erotic intensities in this scene, however, is that the optics are overwhelmingly heterosexual, even though there are most certainly a diversity of intimacies on the beaches. Qian Hui Tan explores how club spaces *become* heterosexual through affect and argues that there are "numerous technologies that are being deployed in order in incite, transmit and sustain (hetero)sexual desire—which is a forceful affective orientation to particular bodies" (Tan 2013, 719). She finds that "sexually affective touch and movement are two ways in which an affectively (hetero)sexualized atmosphere can be sustained" (Tan 2013, 721). Indeed, as hetero games finish on the beaches, pumping music, flowing alcohol, and fantasies of Thailand support bodies to move together, get close, and touch. Music is paramount to these affective charges and is a key part of the erotic heterosexual beach assemblage. While often thought about in the abstract, music is material: sound waves bump against bodies, and vibrations move within the assemblage to encourage relations (Henriques 2010). I often noticed how throughout the evenings, the musical intensity would build to a climax and people's bodies would follow—from slower, quieter, less bass-heavy EDM (electronic dance music) to faster tempos, more well-known songs, and much heavier bass lines at the end; bodies would move from single entities sharing a feeling to jumbled mixtures of grinding pelvises, embracing arms, and frantic legs bouncing to the beats. The effects of the buildup of sexual energy throughout the night created "an infectious energy that can get sexually provocative, its throbbing beats arousing the movement of rhythmically gyrating bodies caught up in the kinesthetics of passion" (Tan 2013, 725). As fire dancers, tourists, and other laborers moved, touched, and played games buoyed by erotic imaginaries of Thailand and centered in heterosexual scripts, they co-created the heterosexual energetic charge of the beach space.

Som viewed the channeling of these hetero affects as an essential role of fire dancers and stated, "So your job is to make people have fun. And doing things that make the man and the girl come to the same group together. They get the girl and then they might be gone, but that's my job. I need to make it fun for them like, 'Oh this party so cool' and for them to meet other people, you know?" During the more informal parts of the evening after the fire show finished, Som would often dress up as a shirtless clown and walk around making balloon animals for men and women, joking with them and complimenting women in what was often interpreted as flirtatious gestures. Som would humorously fashion penis balloons for female revelers, which would garner laughter and sexual jokes. Other dancers would often tickle female tourists and run away giggling in a flirtatious joke that made them appear shy, although this is a very specific technique of engagement. Fire dancers are one component in this assemblage building the crowd and arousing affects. Som, like Nah, did not see his role as flirting with women but rather as adding to the sexual flows already present to ensure that tourists' desires for erotic adventure were fulfilled. Creating possibilities for coupling and working with these affective flows of heterosexual desire help to ensure tourists are having a good time so they will stay at the bar and spend money.

These various elements—alcohol, movement, fire dancers, sound, games, touch, media, tourists, and imaginaries—combine to create an assemblage in which heterosexual coupling is a tendency and that comes to feel more like an expectation than a norm. In fact, I was approached by tourist men so many times during beach parties that it was difficult to build relationships with female tourists and fire dancers. That I was alone, and that I desired *not* to be coupled, was of great concern to tourist men. I used to play a game to see how long it would take for a man to approach me at the beach bars. I would watch men circle my table where I was viewing the show. They would gain confidence and eventually come to sit with me and ask why I was alone. Even when I explained that I was doing research, many insisted on sitting with me and even helping me when I was photographing dancers. While many Thais warned me of the apparent dangers of the island mafia families and fire dancers, the most uncomfortable and dangerous encounters I have had throughout my years in Thailand have been with intoxicated *farang* men. As it turns out, they are also a danger to fire dancers, who must be masters at controlling erotic energies lest they result in affective, and often violent, ruptures.

Agro Affects

"Did it get agro down at the beach last night?" my friend would ask during mornings when we sipped our coffee together on the porch of the guesthouse he owned on Koh Phi Phi. Darren, a *farang* who had lived on Phi Phi for over ten years, worried about how aggressive the male tourists were with Thai and Burmese workers; indeed, stories of stabbings and guns being drawn to ward off obnoxious *farang* were well known on the small island. "Agro" in this context referred to the behavior by (typically) white men at bars and clubs who aggressively try to pick up women and who become aggressive toward other men. Research complements these observations. Tan notes that "the dance floor often translates into 'hunting grounds' for male clubbers impelled to secure a girl by the social pressure of having to perform an aggressive masculinity, and this is compounded by a fiery urge

FIGURE 2.3.   Dancers playing with tourists as part of the show, Koh Samui.

of lust" (2013, 726). I often witnessed this hunting, which was made more urgent by the hetero necessities of the beach, and was hunted numerous times, sometimes aggressively. One man at a bar on Koh Phi Phi watched me for an entire evening as I danced with the bartenders who worked there and whom I had come to know well. He never came up to dance with me but just watched, well into the early hours of the morning. At one point, and in his field of vision, a different *farang* man approached me and started dancing. He became aggressive, charged over, and pushed him out of the area. Overall, I found tourist men to be quite aggressive during these parties, frequently coming up to me, joining my space, and sometimes rubbing up against my body without permission. Indeed, even telling men, and especially white men, what I was researching garnered uncomfortableness on their part. Many responded by suggesting that I was really only interested in having sex with fire dancers and that this was not a "real" focus for a research project.

These behaviors result from *farangs*' inferior masculinities vis-à-vis the powerful male fire dancers who were able to participate with women and enact a *nak leng* masculinity in ways *farang* cannot in these spaces (Malam 2008). Fire dancer Nu explained this, stating, "If you hold the fire, you feel like you are the king. People watching you feel like, 'Oh! He is holding the thing that I am scared of.' You know what I mean? 'He handles the thing that I'm afraid of, that's so strong!'" This aspect of being able to handle danger, to play with it, and to manipulate it made Nu feel powerful. Som, who was somewhat wary of *farang* men, expressed that fire dancing gave him a sense of power and control over them, explaining, "I think they can't do things like me. Really. That's how I feel. And sometimes I see a beautiful girl look at me. With fire you are controlling people's eyes. Ya, when you do fire people are watching you. You can control them." There is a sense of dominance that fire dancers feel on the beaches that is often not afforded them in other spaces. They must, however, carefully strike a balance among engaging *farang* desires and showcasing their power, all while ensuring that "agro" affects do not spin wildly out of control.

While *farang* men are also invited onto the stage during the shows, it is rare to see a dancer spin fire around a man, having him lean back, enveloping and protecting him as fire dancers do with tourist women. What is more common is to have a man come up and sit in a chair and hold a cigarette in his mouth as a dancer tightly winds the *poi* to spin it in a small circle and light his cigarette. What also happens during this trick is that as the male tourist's head is tilted back, a fire dancer will begin to spin the chains of fire on the man's genitals. The tourist reacts with fear but is completely paralyzed, as any movement means his genitals will be burned; the tourist is fully under the control of the male fire dancer. These acts put the *farang's* genitals and masculinity in danger by the dancer, who holds all the power in this encounter, a power that is displayed for everyone at the bar. What becomes clear through these performances is that fire dancers differentially channel affects for *farang* women and men.

The erotic desires that circulate on the beaches must be carefully controlled as they can also elicit jealousy and rage. In speaking about the attraction of fire dancers, Nah explained,

> I don't know why it's like that. Even before when I worked, my girlfriend said the same thing, you know? When you do fire, you sweat, you do your moves, and I don't know haha! I'm not a girl. I don't think this way when I perform. I don't show off too much, but some styles of fire spinner, they do—they show their muscles, you know, and of course they are very attractive. But, like I say, I put my heart in the customer first to see how they feel because sometimes if I go to get tips, if I go to the girls too much, the guys start to, you know, get jealous haha! If a guy and a girl are watching, after the show, you approach the guy first and ask if he wants a picture.

Nah balanced on a precarious line to ensure that he engaged women but never too much. He also related his way of "not showing off" to keeping one's ego low so that he may use the affective technique described previously—of putting his heart in their heart—to attempt to feel with the male tourists to manage such affects. Nah carefully controlled his gestures and bodily performances to mitigate the circulation of jealousy, which could impact his earnings and lead to difficult encounters. For many dancers, nights can devolve into affective ruptures that can turn violent, embarrassing, and challenging.

Nu shared his experiences with the jealous affects of tourist men:

> I had one guy come up when we were spinning in the party. He came and took his pants off and he put his bum next to the fire, and his girlfriend took a picture of him. And we are on the stage. Then he came again and took his penis out and his girlfriend took another picture of him. That was the second time. The third time, we had a seat next to the stage, and he came to our area. He took a seat and then his girlfriend came and sat with the five of us. And he took his penis out again and held his penis and took a picture again. You don't know how rude people are when they are drunk and on holiday and feel like nobody knows them here. They think like, "No one knows me. I can do whatever I want. I am free. I will leave this country." So, they can be super rude! I had a guy that came beside the fire. I stood and then I felt water close to my leg and then I turned, and he was standing and peeing next to me. He tried to pee on me!

While Nu's experiences are troubling, I was not surprised, and I shared some of the behavior I had witnessed from *farang* men as they tried to assert their dominance on the beaches. At a bar on Koh Samui, for instance, no matter how many times the fire dancers asked people to stay behind a rope barrier, which was there to protect everyone during the fire games, tourist men continued to lean on it, try to go under it, go over it, and hop the line to get into the center when it was someone else's turn. During a performance at this same bar, a group of three white men entered the performance space uninvited and attempted to dance *with* the fire dancers, who looked on confused and unsure of what to do. A small crowd formed around the tourist men, and they relished in the attention they were receiving as they drew attention away from the fire dancers. Somewhat forced to engage with them, the fire dancers poured kerosene around the three men and lit it so the *farang* could do their own mini show. I only ever saw men exhibit this type of behavior.

Nu responded to my stories and his own experiences by explaining, "It's about jealousy. It's about that feeling. But I'm not talking about if they are good or bad people, I'm talking about an effect of the mind. Jealousy just comes." Jealousy would suddenly erupt on the beaches and produce these bizarre acts and, sometimes, violence. Stories abound of *farang* men getting beaten and even killed by Thais, and anybody who has been around long enough knows that *farang* often provoke this aggression. During my stay on Phi Phi, *farang* robbed all the alcohol from our Thai neighbor's fridge, threatened the mafia boss of the island, illegally entered the guesthouse where I was staying and ran through the hallways, and got into many violent encounters with other tourists. Pit, a Thai woman who co-owned the guesthouse with Darren where I stayed, would often shake her head and shrug off these incidents, saying, "*Farang* want to show power."

Nu found humorous ways to respond to such behavior during his performances. For the tourist who continued to expose himself, Nu did the following:

> So, he did this three times [exposed himself.] So, I walked up to him and say, "Hey, I think you need the last picture with your clothes off." He was drunk, so I said, "You take off your clothes, be naked, take the picture with us and then you just go home." So, he got naked. I took his clothes, dipped them into the kerosene and burned them with the fire. Poof! Haha! He was naked and had to go back home haha! And all the people they saw. There were a lot of people at the party. And the noise it comes from the party "Yaaaaa!" because they saw that we tried to handle him in a good way.

I asked Nu if he had similar experiences with female tourists and he explained, "No, women are different. Women will come to you like 'haa haa' [panting sexually and wobbling like they are drunk] like this. But I do not drink, so when I see people drunk, for me it's ugly. Come on, like you are human, we can sit, speak, and get to know each other. That is the better way. For men it is that they are jealous when they see all the girls watching. So, they will act differently." For Nu, while part of his role is to generate and channel energies that ensure people are having fun, there was a limit when erotic desires and jealousy ruptured through the assemblage in ways that were uncomfortable. "Do you still have to be nice to them?" I asked, to which Nu responded, "No. I just cut communication fast like, 'Oh sorry I'm working. Thank you, thank you.' I try to make myself like this [puffs out his chest and closes his body posture]. It is already a sign that I have closed myself off. I give a sign [he turns with his body away from me], you see? I close myself. Ya, and they understand the sign." The freedom, abandon, and relative anonymity that travel provides to tourists can become an affective locus that spins out of control and causes harm. In the discussion above, Nu describes the ways in which he managed emotion through the corporeal by closing himself and, in the case of the *farang* man who was exposing himself, reasserting his power in the space to the laughter of the crowd.

Like Nu, Nah also engaged in emotional management to keep these undesired affects in check and again referenced that an artist's ability to feel *with* the audience and establish a moral connection can help alleviate these issues:

The technique I use to do my show is also what I use in life—I put my heart in their heart to see how they feel. I pretend to be them. So, it means that we cannot choose how we are born or our culture. Even myself, I am thirty years old. I look back on my past and how I've become, and I've seen other people how they've become, so I cannot blame them if they have bad behavior. You know, it's how they were born. If we understand that we just feel more like, "Ok, I feel pity but I don't hate you."

For Nah, the same way an artist works to connect with the audience, and emotionally move them can be transferred to moments on the brink of rupture to soothe people and attempt to understand their own perspectives, desires, and emotions. Nah's technique is very much rooted in Buddhist-inspired moralized emotional practices of acceptance (*tham jai*) and detachment (*ploy wang*) so that he can remain calm (*jai yen*), a highly valued affective demeanor (Cassaniti 2014). Nah moved affectively closer to people in an effort to not be angry at tourists for poor behavior, which would affect his own emotionality and thus what he is able to circulate on the beaches as part of his labor.

The affective labor of fire dance is not a unidirectional flow. Rather, it is part of an assemblage of bodies, histories, media, sounds, desires, and imaginaries that coalesce on the tourist beaches. At every moment, fire dancers are assessing the most minute energetic shifts in the atmosphere to respond appropriately and reproduce desires, manage affects, and engage with tourists through their work. Their ability to direct and shape the intensities makes fire dance a poignant site to reconsider conceptualizations of affective labor that have primarily focused on unidirectional and subject-centered flows of emotion. For fire dancers, energies can be named—such as fun, orgasmic, free, or jealous—yet they also flow among porous bodies to materialize in different ways. Energies can be brought to consciousness and articulated but also exist as intersubjective and free-floating material that moves among bodies, affecting them. Their work involves the management of emotions (Hochschild 2003), but these emotions are not contained by bodies. A collective self permeates their understandings, which is opposed to a Eurocentric idea of the self as independent and emotional life as interiorized. Nah's notion of "putting my heart in their heart" exhibits these principles precisely; he can embody a song with tourists as he dances to feel with them and then change as needed to ensure that the right intensities are built for all.

Fire dancers not only articulate an astute ability to work with intensities but also appeal to affect as a mechanism that intervenes in perceptions that deem fire art as deviant and devalued beach labor. Their abilities to create emotional connections with tourists—through the charm of equipment, the movement of their toys, and inviting people to feel the music with them—are upheld as evidence of relationships that are more than economic exchange and are affective relationalities laden with morality. Developing emotional, rather than monetary, relations is saturated by incommensurabilities and attachments that never fully disappear. "Making tourists happy" and putting one's "heart to the audience" are also valuable tools for increasing tips and earning power. The affective labor of fire dancers is not only about their work with tourists but also a technique of management through which they grapple with their positionalities as dancers laboring within tourist economies.

FEELING ART AND THE LABOR OF SHARING

I got off the bus on the far outskirts of Bangkok in a market in Bang Bua Tong. Pi Neung, one of the original Thai fire dancers and the master teacher of many current Thai fire dancers, arrived in a taxi to bring me back to his home for our interview. He greeted me and, as custom, asked if I would like anything to eat. I kindly declined and let him know that I brought food for us to share. We got in the taxi, and he said almost immediately that the "spirit of juggling" had been lost. When we arrived at his small home, a large concrete structure that was sparsely furnished and full of fire art memorabilia, the conversation on the lost spirit continued. He took out some photos of the early days of fire art, back in the 2000s, and I spotted a younger Pi Neung at a park in Bangkok I knew well. He nostalgically recounted how he and a group of friends used to gather in Santichaiprakarn Park to "play" juggling together but how changes ushered in through tourist economies had destroyed the ethos he felt underpinned the movement practice and the community he had built.

The Spirit of the Park

Originally from Nakhon Si Thammarat in the South of Thailand, Pi Neung was among the first Thais to start doing flow art. He learned from American tourists on the island of Koh Chang in the early 1990s, where he had been working in a hotel. They used to play together on the beaches, and he related that one of his American friend's girlfriends gave him his first set of juggling balls, which he kept and brought out to show me. Pi Neung marked this informal way of learning and the act of giving as important to the art form; they were forms of sharing (*baeng pan*), he explained, that helped people form the relations that underpinned what Pi Neung called the "spirit of juggling."[1]

After seeing so many tourists playing with different objects on Koh Chang, because flow art was quite popular at that time, Pi Neung moved to Bangkok to try to earn a living making and selling the equipment on the backpacker strip of Khao San Road. This district, a tourist hub filled with bars, hostels, and shops, allowed him to form many new friendships as he sold his equipment. Just a ten-minute walk from Khao San is Santichaiprakarn Park—a quiet space near the Chao Phraya River enjoyed by Thais, expats, and tourists—where Pi Neung and newly made flow art friends would go to play juggling. It would become a hub for flow art in Bangkok, and the group that formed there was the first in Thailand to start doing fire art as an organized practice. In the 2000s, the group used to practice and have weekly fire shows in the park, and many went daily to play and simply hang out with each other. They were a mix of French, American, Canadian, and Japanese expats, tourists, and Thais who came together organically and eventually formed a tight-knit community. Tourists who did flow art in their own countries would stop by, often teaching and sharing their knowledge. As a core group formed, Pi Neung, along with some of his *farang* friends, began to advertise weekly free Juggle Jams, and he still had one of the posters from these events, which he took out to show me. Some of the original dancers were still active in Thailand at the time of fieldwork, and the park continues to be a meeting ground for flow artists who find themselves in Bangkok, although there are significantly fewer people and no longer a core group.

Playing and learning at the park in the early days were based around a system of noneconomic exchange that Pi Neung and other dancers from this lineage referred to as sharing (*baeng pan*). As the flyer for Juggle Jams asserted, it was a place to "come and enjoy, relax, share skills, instruction available. All ages and skill levels welcome." People would learn with each other, and Pi Neung, who was the most advanced, came to be known as the master teacher. He never charged people for lessons, although he expected that they would purchase equipment from him. What was important about the park, for Pi Neung, was the type of sociality that this sharing fostered, a feeling of community—the spirit—that he felt had been lost.

Pi Neung nostalgically shared how this change happened as the genre became a performance done for tourists in return for money. For Pi Neung, this ushered forth new competitive desires that began to permeate the group and their willingness to share.

AUTHOR: [Looking at a magazine article about the original group] Is this you in park?

PI NEUNG: Yes, Santichaiprakarn Park

AUTHOR: Why did everyone learn there?

PI NEUNG: Ya, that was like a juggling park, you know? Before, we were there every day! Now there are no people.

AUTHOR: Yes, sometimes I go there and there are only few jugglers, but not every day.

PI NEUNG: I think maybe the spirit is gone from there. Ya, the spirit.

AUTHOR: What was the spirit like in the days when you were there?

PI NEUNG: It was very good for me. After competition came, it was very bad. When we started getting performance jobs, we would go all together as a group, and we would share the money. Soon after, we were with an agency, and they wanted to give out separate jobs, like "You go to this one, you go to this one" [perform at different places]. And after that, the group didn't really stay with me. They separated. They gave their business cards to agencies and then they got their own jobs.

Pi Neung related how when the dancers he trained and shared with were offered monetary incentives, they left him to go and do private gigs. Indeed, dancers whom I met in the South had left the group in the mid-2000s to go to the islands where fire dance was becoming a lucrative job in the tourist economy. Doing so, after Pi Neung had shared so much, hurt him, and he expressed, "They joined with me, but why don't they want to share with me? Not only one time, but they came with me many times. After they got their own company, when they go to the park they never say hello to me; they see me like I am against them."

Pi Neung was particularly disheartened when he discovered that some of these dancers were charging people for lessons: "Some of the people I was teaching for free, but when they taught people, they sold the lessons, like saying, 'If you want to learn, it is ten hours for 3,000 baht.' But I gave this to them and taught them almost every day—for no baht! They did not support me. I never made a website to advertise lessons and learning; I only sold people equipment so they could come to learn. If I gave a lesson, I would say you have to buy equipment from me and I will teach you what you want to know." This discomfort with monetary exchange is in line with what Ben Tausig (2014) finds is a centering of mutuality and reciprocity, qualities that constitute musical relationships in Thailand as moral. Morality in a teacher-student relationship is especially crucial, and students are often considered to be indebted to teachers forever.[2] While money is still very much part of musical worlds and relationships, desires for profitability are carefully negotiated by musicians in relationship with audiences and teachers. This is not unlike how fire dancers in chapter 2 likened affective exchange with the audience as key to moral fire artistry.

In defining different temporal periods in fire art history, Pi Neung marks his moral world. His reference to the ushering in of competition relates how juggling migrated from a kin economy, built through the mutuality of sharing, to a more market-oriented system (Wilson 2004). Once competition and the prospects of making money entered the park group, the moral systems of social exchange, among student-teacher and among kin, were disrupted for Pi Neung. However, a dimension of Pi Neung's Juggle Jams and park hangouts also surrounded his desire to sell flow art equipment, which rooted these sessions in market exchange. Yet Pi Neung felt that the movement of juggling to a performance genre and a commodity form in Thailand brought a sense of competition that disrupted the relations and sociality being built through sharing—the spirit.

Pi Neung related that as fire art became a business, particular aesthetics of flow art were also changed. He explained that competition was driven by a person's desire to be what he called a performer—that is, someone who wants to make money. He felt that a desire to do flow art for increased concentration, coordination, and making social relationships was more authentic to the genre. For Pi Neung, the spirit of juggling emerged as people came together with intentions for relationship building and to learn more about the nature of one's body and mind. He pointed to the quote from the book *The Complete Juggler* (Finnegan, Strong, and Jacobs 1987) on the Juggle Jam poster he had pulled out earlier to explain this ethos: "Almost anyone can juggle. It's not an art form reserved for circus people but is a physically and mentally relaxing form of recreation which can help you discover and nurture your innate coordination. . . . It can have the same calming effect on your spirit as playing or listening to good music. For many, juggling is a form of meditation, or integrating mind, body and soul (Finnegan 1987, Finnegan cited on Thai Juggle Jam flyer)." Pi Neung believed that those who had left him alone in the park to pursue jobs in the tourist industry corrupted this ethos by focusing on what he referred to as "tricks," a flashy performance style that he felt emerged from desires for money and to bolster one's ego. These principles, for Pi Neung, were embodied and a dancer's "true" desires were revealed in how the dancer moved.

He explained that when learning, one's mind must be free of competition, and one must learn from the way one's body moves naturally: "Always there are people that want to be the best or something like that, you know? But the way they start is not the same. They start by competition. I start by nature." As he showed me ways to improve my *poi* technique in his front garage that had been converted into a living space, he had me go back to simply tossing a ball from one hand to the other. We spent a long time unlearning the tendency to forcibly throw it. The easiest way, in fact, is to toss the ball gently up in the air and let it fall, the natural way. He said, "It is against nature! You have to learn with your body. That comes with your nature." What emerges from the natural way of moving the ball is a somewhat controlled and yet free-flowing gliding of the ball that is graceful and calm and appears effortless. He countered this aesthetic by showing me great exertion, force, and the tightness he associated with what he called the "fast spinning" and "tricks" born from a desire to perform rather than learn and share with others. He stated, "I think for performers it is that feeling of 'Ahhhh I have to spin fast' [motions with his arms quickly]. This is an art that you have to open for everyone. If they understand this spirit, they won't think, 'Oh, this is difficult and I never can.' You have to learn and try from your nature."

Knowing that he had performed a few times with his group at the park, I asked if some performers were able to keep the spirit alive, and he related,

> When beginning, I was not thinking about that because then there was no competition. We played what we knew. Nature. We put music on and would spin and follow the music: if the music was fast, we would spin fast; if the music was slow, we would spin slow, move slow. Now, they all do tricks. It's no longer about the art or story in the *poi* or staff. On the beach, Myanmar dancers only spin fast fast fast fast fast. For me, you have to learn everything. That means you are a juggler. Not only *poi*—you have to know staff, diablo, contact ball. You have to learn everything because they use the same feeling.

Pi Neung's remarks are much like Som's in chapter 2 and express that one must know many pieces of equipment to draw out the essence of each toy. There is a slippage, however, between speaking about performers, whom Pi Neung marks as those with competitive desires, and the Burmese dancers in the new generation. Pi Neung's rendering of those with the spirit and those without gathers wider fears and discourses about changing tourist economies and labor patterns that have made securing jobs and resources difficult for Thai dancers. Pi Neung expanded on this later during the interview and explained that it was likely the Burmese who had triggered this increased competition that his park dancers had succumbed to:

> PI NEUNG: Myanmar workers came a few years ago. Maybe four or five years ago. Not before. Before, it was Thai people. That's why it is like this—because competition.
>
> AUTHOR: Why did it change when the Myanmar workers came?

PI NEUNG: They only know about fire spinning, you know? Like spin
very fast [he motions with his arms quickly]. For me, after that, I
didn't want to spin very fast.

Perhaps the Burmese laborers began arriving as his students left Bangkok for the
islands, and thus fire dance became more competitive than it once was. However,
what Pi Neung is documenting and expressing are his perception and issues with
the transformation of a communal, participatory art form into a presentational
performance that is integrated into tourism in a more market-oriented way.

Money had always been exchanged in the park for equipment, yet sharing became the principle through which Pi Neung developed affective ties and defined kin economies. As fire dance became a commodity form, an aesthetic of
fastness emerged, and Pi Neung felt left behind. I had been introduced to Pi
Neung by some of his former students who had realized the earning potential
of fire dance and left Bangkok to make money on the islands. Many became incredibly successful dancers, but, as they explained, their master, Pi Neung, had
not fared so well. I was encouraged by them to give a donation to Pi Neung for
sharing his knowledge with me because of the difficult economic circumstances
he was in. At the end of our interview, as I attempted to give him the money, he
insisted that in exchange he give me a piece of equipment he had made. He said
that even though he sometimes struggled for rent, he had enough (*pho phiang*).

After speaking extensively about the tensions of money in the scene, I felt uncomfortable even offering, and I sensed that he, too, was uncomfortable. Pi
Neung went to his front room and gifted me a set of Kevlar fire *poi*. It was an
exchange I felt may have been like those in the early days, and one he felt was
essential among flow artists. As I got ready to leave, I asked if he would ever play
again in the park. He replied, "Not the park—it has changed. Because now when
they come, there are many groups that are separate. They go there, and the others
they go and sit there [he motions with his hands to different groups in different
areas]. They are not feeling together about juggling."

Pi Neung's account of fire dancing invokes many of the common tensions,
hopes, fears, and anxieties of dancers that revolve around increased economic
pressures and a movement away from the hiring of teams to more dispersed and
neoliberal modalities where dancers must sell themselves to a bar. Pi Neung
grappled with the politics of this changing tourism industry and emerging migration patterns that shifted flow art over the years. He yearned for a time when
he felt the intention of dancers was centered in the intimate labor of creating
community such as at Santichaiprakarn Park. Of course, Pi Neung was not removed from the market economies and the competition he struggled with, and
he was part of generating the industry. His story and nostalgic longings demon-

strate attachments, affects, and moralities as, at times, incommensurable with people's needs and desires for money. Pi Neung is still renowned in Thailand and considered the father of the first generation of Thai fire dancers. I did not meet a dancer who was not, in some way, connected to his lineage.

Sharing (*Baeng Pan*)

I took a *motocy* taxi uphill along the winding road away from a large tourist strip on the island of Koh Samui. Tucked away on a small piece of land was an open-air structure filled with flow art equipment, mirrors, and *motocys* parked outside. The *motocy* driver dropped me off for the first time at the fire art center, the only of its kind in Thailand, and Nah, the co-owner, came to greet me. We performed an awkward dance of greeting on this first encounter as we assessed which one of us was higher on the social hierarchy. Nah is a teacher, so he was above me, but I am slightly older than Nah. We both awkwardly *wai*'d each other at the same time, although my position as a student would be firmly established in the coming days.[3] He welcomed me inside, and after some discussion I sat at the small bar on a stool. He pointed to a picture hanging on the wall of a masked man who looked like a circus performer—"My master," exclaimed Nah. The masked man was Pi Neung.

Nah was in his mid-thirties, and with the help of his Swiss *farang* girlfriend, Anik, he set up a studio space for fire artists on Koh Samui. Koh Samui is the most developed island, and it is served by an international airport. The tourism industry there is extensive, with many high-end resorts. Koh Samui also has a large expat community from North America, Europe, and increasingly China whose members work as event and wedding planners, bar co-owners, dive shop operators, musicians, and managers at resorts. The fire art scene caters to a wide range of events, and there are many Thai and Burmese dancers as well as *farang* fire performers who labor as part of a working holiday. Thai dancers felt that the influx of laborers from Myanmar had disrupted the scene on Koh Samui, much like on other islands. Because the Burmese dancers worked for less money, Thai dancers were losing income, and ethnonational tensions on the island were palpable. Nah sought to standardize pricing on Koh Samui to mitigate these disputes and ensure that all dancers were paid fairly. He attempted to organize with all Thai and Burmese fire dancers to create a type of union and agree on a standardized amount to charge bar owners. While not all dancers agreed and there was still much undercutting, Nah managed to establish a large group of dancers to create what he characterized as an agency housed at the fire art center—an outdoor, open air studio space. He took a small percentage from performances, mostly for the upkeep of the space, and distributed the rest to the dancers based on their skill level. With the help of his girlfriend, who is trained in marketing, Nah sought to ensure the center had a reputation of high-level of artistry and professionalism, which they referred to as luxury.

Nah and others at the fire art center who were from Pi Neung's lineage and had learned at the park with him considered flow art to be foremost a participatory practice. Like Pi Neung, they felt that the early days of flow art in the park had a different feeling than its current iteration in tourist economies. Pi Tha, now in his forties, was at the center one day. He no longer danced, but Nah was trying to help him make some money farming, and he would come to teach at the center in exchange. Pi Tha had left the group to perform on the islands in the mid-2000s and related, "It felt different then. We would play, eat, and even sleep together. The whole park, there were so many people." Nah agreed:

> Yes, because at that time we loved it as hobby. And now it's become part of our job. Before, you could speak with your friend like, "Hey, today we will go busking and grab a beer." Now, no. All of us are busy, have responsibilities, and we have to think seriously. Most of the artists are from many different places. If they start to make their own show, they start to hate each other. Well, it's not like hating each other, but kind of like competition, you know? It's normal. But I opened here and it's more like sharing. Ya, sharing.

Like Pi Neung, Nah described the notion of sharing as an antidote to competition, central to the feeling of the park and an essence that he sought to foster in his fire art center. Nah and Pi Tha felt that the move to tourist-centered performances brought a sense of competition to the fire art scene; the pull of opportunities in the tourist market economy supplanted systems of sharing and structures of performance where people might busk together informally but not as a main source of income. The center was discussed as being fundamentally run through modes of sharing as a way to mark a line between capitalist and kin economies, even while it was fully immersed in and dependent on transnational neoliberal capitalism to survive. Sharing, however, became the mechanism through which Nah and the other dancers attempted to recapture the spirit of those early days.

When I first visited in 2016, the fire art center was a twenty-minute *motocy* ride from the bustle of the large tourist beach road. The center was set back from the road in a grassy open area. Its large, red roof contained an open concrete space filled with flow art equipment, colorful decorations, flow art memorabilia, stools, a couch, and large mirrors for people to practice in front of. The space outside of the structure was also used to practice and contained a mirror, picnic tables, and a hammock. The area was quiet, green, and lush, which was a stark contrast to the

FIGURE 3.1.   Fire art equipment at the fire art center on Koh Samui.

tourist area where I stayed. The center was modeled off a *farang*-run guesthouse in the hippie tourist enclave of Pai, a small town in the North of Thailand. The guesthouse was a business venture meant to attract traveling yogis and artists that largely catered to white tourists craving a back-to-nature feel, yoga lessons, and access to flow art equipment. Nah, however, adapted this model as he felt that the guesthouse in Pai was set up with an intention to make money, a motivation he viewed as lacking, and in contradistinction to, the affective relations he wished to establish.

> AUTHOR: How did you get the idea for this place?
> NAH: Pai Flow House, but mine is different. I felt uncomfortable there. Nobody spoke to me.
> AUTHOR: Why?
> NAH: It's more of a business.
> AUTHOR: Did they not know you are one of the most famous artists in Thailand!?
> NAH: Those people, if they don't see you have a skill, they give no respect. They didn't see me do it. If you see someone on the street or at a show, like "Wow!" and you give them respect because of what they can do. They didn't see me do it. It was 400 baht just to go there. I don't have that money. Here [the center] it is all about artists.

Nah felt that the socioeconomic divisions that limited access and a sense of camaraderie manifested because that guesthouse was set up as a business. Nah viewed his fire art center, however, as being developed with a different intention. He differentiated how his nonbusiness approach is more central to fostering artists. Capturing and re-creating a particular feeling of the early days is interconnected with dancers' attempts to legitimize their practice as art; artistry and sharing were co-constitutive at the center, and the moral lines surrounding economic versus affective motivations were once again animated.

During my time at the center in 2016, there was a core group of seven Burmese dancers and six Thai dancers who went almost every day. Two of these dancers were a couple, Dao and Song. Dao was the only female fire dancer at the center, and she was among the last remaining female Thai dancers in the country. They were not original park dancers but from the second generation and taught by Nah and others who studied under Pi Neung. The seven Burmese dancers were the youngest and were trained and taught by Nah. He managed to secure them a very well-paid contract at one of the biggest bars on the island, where they danced as a team each evening. Other dancers who frequented the center were not necessarily fire artists but performers who entertained tourists at hotels, mostly doing hip-hop routines. Anik, Nah's partner, was not at the center regularly, as most of her work involved behind-the-scenes planning. Nah, however, was there every day. On some days, tourist flow artists or *farang* performers who worked on the island would stop by and join in. Other times, a Thai dancer friend from another island might come to stay for a few days to share in teaching and practice.

As Nah expressed on my first visit and multiple times after, the center was "a place for artists" and fostered a type of belonging that was not centered on ethnonational or cultural identification but rather on shared intentions to do fire art together. Indeed, the set of world flags strung around the roof was a reminder of this ethos. What was important to Nah was that dancers practiced intensively to showcase themselves as artists rather than beach boys. The day would start around 2:00 p.m. as people would arrive on their *motocys*, often sharing the bike with a fellow dancer. Fire dancers typically work late into the evening, and thus the rhythm of the day began in the late afternoon. As people arrived, they typically would sit on the couch or the beanbag chairs as their bodies woke, snack on some food, chat, and play on their phones. An hour or so later, someone would begin to practice outside in the back or in front of the big mirror under the covered area. One person would grab one of the toys, which were usually strewn about the space, and start. As if all in sync, others would join until everyone was playing and practicing together. This sort of play with intermittent periods of relaxation and chatting went on every day in almost the exact same manner until around 8:00 p.m., when people generally left to head to their nightly gigs.

FIGURE 3.2. Dancers practicing at the fire art center on Koh Samui.

FIGURE 3.3. Fire dance team, Koh Samui.

Of prime importance was that members fostered a motivation to learn and do fire dance based in sharing—with fellow center members and with audiences. For Nah, this focus upheld and fostered the noncompetitive ideal that he felt marked his center as different. Although the dancers at the center were very much situated in the tourist industry and all performed for money, everyone taught each other and shared their knowledge freely. Sharing was invoked daily to reference how money, duties, learning, and teaching operated through communal responsibilities and aspirations. Given that I was initially considered somewhat of a tourist, I was asked to pay for lessons, but I was soon incorporated into the sharing system. After two lessons, in which Nah showed me some basic moves and techniques, I was then told not to pay, but to learn from sharing with others at the center.

I would often stand outside where there is a large cement floor, a mirror, and a picnic table, and as I began to practice, another dancer would come over to share a move with me. I would still contribute the forty-baht center fee, which was required of tourists and performers who had secure jobs, but during my final months, Nah encouraged me to stop doing so. Sharing also involved an even division of duties to maintain the studio space, assist with promotion, and organize shows. There was not a great surplus for upkeep, so all were expected to clean, help build new parts, gather materials and equipment, and maintain the space. Performances also had shared aspects even for those not dancing. If there was a big show or event, dancers who were not performing were expected to help in planning, taking photos, driving people, and providing refreshments. This sharing system operated quite smoothly, and even tourists who stopped by to jam or to learn were encouraged to share their knowledge with others in the space. Because I was the least experienced and thus did not have a repertoire of techniques to share, I was expected to share in different ways. I was often asked to clean or help with paid workshops that the center held for the children of expats. I helped to edit documents and biographies, took photos and videos, cleaned performance sites, and carried equipment.

The center was a space very intentionally attempting to create a system in opposition to market exchange even while it was fully enmeshed in and dependent on transnational capital to survive. While the dancers shared together to prepare for paid performances and charged particular people for lessons, it was clear that money was seen to be somewhat of a corrupting force; it could create competition and needed to be carefully managed. The ideal of non-economic sharing was not only an aspect of more sociocentric modalities of living but also guided by Theravada Buddhist moralities that consider worldly attachments to be a source of suffering that can affect one's rebirth.

Nah told me the following story of the Buddha one day as we sat outside on the grass—one of our only formal interviews where we were not practicing together or riding around the island, Nah's preferred method for sharing knowledge with me:

> The Buddha has one rule: if you are a monk and you study until you get power that makes you more than human, you cannot show this power if it's not important. But one day he showed this power to open another dimension—paradise and hell—to humans so they all can see and so they would believe it's real. After that he went up to see his mother for many months. People on the earth missed him so much, so they created the statue from wood. Every day, the people would go and pray. And the Buddha came back, and he saw the people doing this and said, "Why do you do that [worship a statue]?" You do that and you don't get anything. You don't get your spirit to be more pure. Because to be pure, for your spirit to be pure, you have to do meditation to silence all the frequencies that you receive so you can know more. For example, so you can see the past, so you can see the future, and before you die your spirit can't be too dirty. When you receive too many material things, you get addicted to them. Material things make your soul more dirty, and you will come back in the same circle after you die. To get out of that, you have to understand, and then you reach another level, and then reach another level until the very top and you will not come back again.

Nah ordained as a monk in his younger years, which most young Thai and Burmese boys do, but this was the only story Nah told of the Buddha, and it communicates important features that structure the moral principles at the center: artists must not become attached to material items or power.

Money is a corrupting attachment in Buddhist thought. The overaccumulation of money beyond one's needs can signify greed and immorality in Thailand. To reconstitute a moral relation with money, those who have larger amounts of resources often perform public acts of donations to temples, to village ordinations, and other initiatives to redistribute wealth and to demonstrate generosity (Reynolds 1990). These redistributions allow one to gain merit (*bun*) in Theravada Buddhist logic. Merit-making (*tham bun*) is central to Thai, as well as Burmese, cosmological beliefs and social life, and it generally involves giving gifts or donations to monks who transfer back cosmological power to laypeople. The merit one is able to gain directly correlates to one's rebirth and is governed by karma (*kam*): the more merit one accumulates, the better one's rebirth.

While merit determines a person's position in the cosmological hierarchy, it also determines one's position in society and is intersected by class politics. Those who are rich, powerful, and generous are thought to have accumulated more merit in past lives and thus have had a better rebirth. However, this means they can also give more freely and perform these acts of merit making (Bowie 1998; Hanks 1962). These ideals are significant in daily life and also influence national moral ideologies and policies. As Arnika Fuhrmann relates, the 1997 Asian financial crisis "prompted renewed engagement with notions of Thai culture and heritage and its profitable integration into political and Buddhist-coded economic programs such as the sufficiency policy. Sufficiency (*khwam pho phieng*) [to have enough] designates a Buddhist-coded notion of economic, political, and affective moderation, or a localized notion of austerity" (2016, 5–6). The policy was laden with sociomoral principles meant to protect Thailand and "rhetorics of paring down, of rationing, and of exhortations to return to quintessentially Thai ways of living had high currency" (Fuhrmann 2009, 224).

Sharing and the distribution of resources at the center are strikingly similar and draw on the same moral principles; indeed, Pi Neung used this exact language when describing that, overall, his life had turned out all right because he had "enough" (*pho phiang*). Money—moving from tourists to Nah and again to dancers—is situated in a moral model that ensures everyone has enough and that dancers do not become too attached to material goods. The center was ultimately a space where money and economic attachments could be cleansed through the creation of moral economies based in sharing. Importantly, the Burmese dancers at the center were also Theravada Buddhists, and thus these principles allowed for solidarities to form around particular moral views, although as will be discussed in chapter 4, ethnonational tensions also emerged through such sharing.

The language and practices at the center contain other threads of Buddhist ideologies surrounding detachment and moderation. For instance, people were never required to "pay" for lessons or for using the studio but were encouraged to give a "donation," a word that directly invokes merit-making rather than economic transactions (Cate 2003). Som, who talked about his large salary and his ability to make a lot of money as a dancer, often described how he redistributed his funds: "I do a lot of busking and give all my money to the temple. I've done this three times already in my life." On another occasion, when he was about to do a tour in China with a circus group, he said that he would be making 60,000 baht, a hefty sum in Thailand. After he returned, he told me he was going to share this with his other teammates who had not been able to go. When I began this research, I planned to pay dancers for their time and the knowledge they would share with me, but this was not welcomed at the center. When Nah, Anik, and I

DAO: Ah! Like trick one, trick two, trick three. My own flow. I can do all these tricks, but I only combine one and I count to three first and then two. Something like that.

AUTHOR: Is this different for every person?

DAO: Ya. Like there is no particular pattern of these tricks. For it to be your own flow, you combine them all in your way. And sometimes when you meet people who are like you, you talk to them. They might share something, and you might share something and now you got a new thing to add. And it keeps adding on.

One day, Dao showed me different ways to combine all the tricks that I knew, and how to move my body in more creative and graceful ways to start a flow. I practiced endlessly trying to transition between moves and turn my body in a circle at the same time. Dao cheered when I finally got the beginning of a flow that was individual to my body—something natural, as Pi Neung had said to me.

Som, on another afternoon, worked with me on a transitional movement called the waterfall and showed me various bodily twists and turns that I could choose from when I executed this trick. After months of practicing, I could go through many of my movements, and I would often think about whose patterns, moves, and help were embodied in my flow; it had small pieces of Dao, Som, Pi Neung, Nah, Jes, and many other dancers. This aesthetic is one that embodies a type of individuality born from relationality. Much like the toys I was to purchase as a gift to the dancers, so that they could all use and touch them, our flow had remnants of all those who had shared with us along our journeys. It was an individual flow full of exchanges and the intimate labor of sharing. Like Pi Neung's rendering of a natural style being the embodiment of a noncompetitive ethos, a slow flow signified not only a person's artistry but the ability to share and thus was viewed as being expressive of one's moral principles and artistry.

Slow flows were positioned in counterdistinction to the fast spinning that Pi Neung referred to at the beginning of the chapter. Spinning fast signified that a dancer was only interested in making money or having access to *farang* rather than fire dancing for the love of making art and sharing it. While fast spinning was often applied to Burmese dancers throughout the scene, Nah attributed this not so much to their ethnonational backgrounds but more so to their young ages—as part of the new generation who lacked experience. He related,

I was the same. Yes. When you are young, your energy is different. When you do *poi* and when you are spinning, you don't see yourself. You don't see yourself and you just go fast fast fast fast fast. And I did the same until one day I saw my video and thought, "Oh! Why so fast? Why do it only fast?" So, I started trying to feel what the customer feels.

> If you just spin and do five moves in five seconds, the audience will not understand a thing. They just see spin spin spin, you know? Of course, it looks fast, looks quick, and looks good. But the audience won't understand a thing about what I'm doing. It's a waste.

Nah felt that through looking at a dancer he could tell which ones had desires for money. He explained, "I can see which performer comes from that. Yes, it's very easy because they have less basic moves. They just come and show only difficult moves, and you cannot find any basic or any simple moves at all, you know? That is, for me, not an artist, and not beautiful."

Interestingly, Zaw, one of Nah's first Burmese students, explained that because of his years studying under Nah he could "play like Nah's style," which he believed differentiated him from other Burmese beach dancers who were not part of the center. When I asked him about the team that performed next to the bar where he worked, he related that they were "very different because our crew has the basics [technique]. They [the other team] learn from YouTube." Zaw used the same discourse that Thai dancers employed to describe Burmese dancers as unskilled and not having flow. Having flow was about being graceful and showcasing the simplicity of moving the body with fire and only carefully interspersing tricks at just the right moment. Doing otherwise was indicative of a high ego and immoral motivations.

Aesthetics at the fire art center had much wider relevance than determining moral affects. The idealization of slow flows over fast spinning and tricks is an engagement with how one takes time with one's body and others, sensing how bodies reach and extend into spaces, how they touch and relate to others. This is inherently political, as through slow flowing and sharing the center dancers attempt to shift relations of power and tensions in the fire dance market economy brought through "fast" touristic capitalism, a parallel between socioeconomic systems and performance aesthetics that cannot go unnoticed (Franko 2002; Kunst 2011; Martin 2011). An embodied ideal of slow moral artistry is an intervention and part of constituting a politics and an economy of sharing that is bodied forth through slow, controlled flows. The slow flows of kin economies and the fast spinning of what fire dancers see as immoral capitalist desires reverberate with wider social rhythms of the everyday that are very much felt, contested, and re-created.

Henri Lefebvre argues that "the rhythm that is proper to capital is the rhythm of producing (everything: things, men, people, etc.) and destroying (through wars, through *progress*, through inventions and brutal interventions, through speculation, etc." (Lefebvre 2004, 5). Capitalism is described as a pattern of accumulation, speed, spread, and proliferation (Harvey 2001; Massey 1994; Tsing

2005). The rhythms of capitalism are disruptively fast, and the ethos of neoliberalism steeped in individual responsibility and the entrepreneurial self fosters a speed that is often experienced alone and disconnected; time becomes a valuable commodity that one uses and spends in line with the market needs. As I listened to Thai inhabitants on multiple islands, I realized that it was not only this lineage of dancers who linked an embodied fastness with immoral desires and competition. The word "fast" was used as a boundary-setting mechanism, much more widely. Tourists moved too fast, drove *motocys* too fast, walked and spoke too quickly, and had bodies that vibrated with stress; they were busy and demanded speed from those who worked in the industry. Indeed, my Thai friends even asked me to slow down and to not rush as I took time to forge relationships with them. The center and Santichaiprakarn Park, where Thai fire art began, were removed slightly from such bustling tourist areas, and dancers positioned these spaces as outside of and resistant to capitalist exchange; these were understood as gathering areas in which people prioritized long, slow days of chatting, sharing food, and exchanging dance moves with others. Sharing in these spaces animated kin economies and forged affective relations that were likely *felt* as more moral, less capitalist, and artistic. This was not only accomplished through teaching each other new tricks; it manifested in the quotidian intimate labor performed among people who shared long periods of time together. Time became valuable not for earning potential but for whom one might be able to connect with and how that relationship could be fostered. These acts changed relationships to time and allowed people to share in a similar daily rhythm, perhaps one that felt slower.

When I first met Jes, he assured me that even though he was thrust into an industry already fully ensconced in the market economy, the feeling of fire art had changed for him after he joined the center:

> One year ago, I didn't know that I am making art because I was only thinking of this for fun or for a way to make money. But if you asked me now, "Do you love it?" I love it. But then, I didn't really know that what I was doing was art. But now I understand. Because every time when I do this, it makes me so happy and comfortable. So, I like fell in love with this and started to understand that it is something I love and like. But one year ago, I didn't know this. I just thought it was something to make good money and do for fun. Before I didn't know about art because I just did it for money. That's it. But now I can feel it.

Jes makes a clear distinction between the feelings of doing art for money and doing it for love, as he says. This was a type of moral artistry that the center fostered, and it was absolutely embodied, felt, and real, despite its complexities and contradictions. The ideal of sharing and the kin relations it constituted became a mechanism through which the lost "spirit" and "feeling" were experienced as renewed, even as dancers were entangled in market economies and desires for money.

The center was a site of solidarity among fire dancers, a space where what is often perceived as an undervalued and heavily commercialized, tourist beach art was reconfigured and reconstituted through aesthetics and systems of sharing. The intimate labor of sharing—technique, duties, and income—created a felt sociality akin to the spirit that Pi Neung spoke of and the feeling of art that Jes and Dao expressed. Slow flows and long days spent together made these connections possible and were a key mechanism through which dancers recreated a sense of community in neoliberal climates that idealize entrepreneurialism, self-sufficiency, accumulation, and market prosperity. Sharing—whether it was through sitting and chatting, eating food together, cleaning the center, or teaching each other fire dance techniques—was, at its core, relational work that rewrote these scripts by ensuring that everyone had enough (*pho phiang*). The intimate labor of sharing was productive of something more than survival, more than the functioning of a center on limited resources or ensuring the longevity and progression of fire art. For the dancers, it generated a felt sociality that helped to manage a discomfort with systems of neoliberal capitalist exchange and the types of attachments this economic system can foster.

Given the contradictions and tensions in these discussions, ideals of slow flows are ways in which dancers negotiate and reposition themselves as moral figures in the landscape of touristic capitalism. Upholding these principles not only allows for spaces and art making to feel differently but perhaps also allows the economic dimension, the flow of money from tourist to dancer, to also feel differently—as a matter of shared relationships through the exchange of affect rather than a chain of production and consumption. While dancers parse out affective relations and monetary exchange, they are intertwined. However, these distinctions are used as affective registers to define their moral worlds, albeit in complex and sometimes contradictory ways. There are tensions embedded in Pi Neung's and the center dancers' idealizations that are never completely resolved. The need for money and the recognition that one's survival is entangled in capitalist markets are ever-present. Theravada Buddhist ideals of detachment and moderation are intertwined with these needs, and thus sharing, and specific types of affective and bodily engagements become sites through which the incommensurability of desires to be moral and the need to participate and survive through tourist market economies as an artist are managed. The center,

modeled off the informal practice among a diverse group of people at Santi-
chaiprakharn Park in the early days, is a place where the enmeshment of fire art
with commodity forms and the greed that fuels ethnonational divisions are
reframed. Sharing provided a system of intercultural and intergenerational relational labor that is unimaginable in other spaces of the tourist industry.

THE AFFINITIVE LABOR OF FREEDOM

I arrived at the new fire art center, which had been recently converted and moved to a different part of the island since I was last there three years earlier. I peeked into a domed structure covered in palm leaf thatch to find Naing and Jes—two fire dancers from Myanmar—and Song, a Thai dancer, helping each other fix the roof. Jes and Song held the scaffolding carefully in place while Naing climbed high. It reminded me of the way they climbed on top of each other's shoulders to perform the intricate holding patterns in their shows. Later that afternoon, I would watch as Song and others practiced with the newly arrived Burmese dancers who were learning how to stay balanced in these challenging poses. Song noticed Naing struggling and climbed up the scaffolding to help. They joked and laughed with each other at the silliness of fixing a roof that continued to leak water in new places. They looked at me, smiled, and proudly exclaimed that they built this new studio space together.

I was always struck by small moments like these, which happened frequently in the space. Thai and Burmese dancers worked and shared together here—something that was rare in the industry more widely. The fire art center was designed by Nah specifically to generate such relations and showcase the utopian and community-building potentials of fire dance. The aesthetic of slow flows discussed in chapter 3 came to symbolize the reinvigoration of kin economies in the midst of touristic capitalism. There were certainly intimate social bonds among people, but the creation of new hierarchies meant that dancers from Myanmar had to carve out their own ways to belong. This chapter highlights the lives, experiences, and practices of the young Burmese team members who trained at the center. I examine how these dancers navigate the entanglement of gender and the politics of belonging at the center and how they create their own communities and moralities against the backdrop of discourses that position them, and the spaces they work within, as deviant.

Artists In-Becoming

While the Burmese dancers at the fire art center participated and belonged as members, they were viewed somewhat differently from the Thai dancers. The Burmese students were positioned as the most junior, partly because of their ages, and thus were lowest on the internal hierarchy. Given that they were the least experienced, Nah felt that he had to teach them to be artists—that is, they were not already fully constituted as the Thai fire artists were considered to be. Echoing sentiments heard across many fieldwork sites, Nah and other center members thought that the Burmese learned too quickly through YouTube videos, and without sharing in a community, because they were motivated to secure an income. Thai dancers felt that they did not have a love of the art form and had to be trained to feel this.

Nah was disheartened by what he felt were the difficult circumstances that these men found themselves in and that created such motivations:

> I see the Thai community of spinners is bigger than before, but it's growing slowly. But, from what I see, they are real artists, Thai spinners. They do this from what they love, not because they come here and do it to survive. In Thailand, it's very hard to find Thai people to do this because you need real people to have this passion to do it. With Burmese people it is easier because they come to Thailand not to be lazy. When they're here, they have to survive and doing fire shows is one of the things that gives good and quick money. And I can find Burmese dancers easily, but to find real artists is not easy. Ya, so technically all my students, I teach them to be artists.

Nah was sympathetic to the Burmese dancers' need to survive. He understood Thais as more natural artists because they could pursue fire dance for noneconomic motivations. The Burmese dancers were viewed as better workers because of their urgent economic needs, but these monetary necessities were thought to create desires and attachments that were corrupting of the type of affective moral artistry Nah wanted to foster. Thus, dancers from Myanmar were positioned as less mature artists-in-becoming who needed Nah's mentorship to foster affects that he considered moral.

Nah explained how he encouraged the Burmese team toward moral artistry. For instance, he took issue with tipping practices on the beaches where the Burmese dancers performed. He felt that it disrupted affective relations with the audience. As he explained in chapter 2, if they received tips too early in a performance it would change their energy. However, he was ambivalent about tipping, more generally. Nah explained,

> If you watch when people go for tips you can see how they react; if they really want money they will go around with the tip box like, "Hello money, money, tip, tip." When people do not give, they just go to another table and get tips, and then go to another table. I don't recommend my students do that. I tell them that the point of the show is to make the audience feel enjoyment. If they want to give you tips, they will give it to you. If they don't give, you just say "Thank you. Hope you enjoy the night." You have to say goodbye, you have to make friends a bit. Even when you do that, sometimes they might walk back and give it to you. You have to make them feel comfortable. If you make a proper show, have respect, smile, and make them feel comfortable, if they do not give, you still give them respect. It makes the audience and even you feel better.

Nah knew that I regularly went to see the Burmese team's nightly shows at the beach bar, and he would sometimes ask me if they had walked around with the tip bucket. I always told Nah that I had to leave before that point, so I was not sure. Of course, the team walked around with the tip bucket every night, from table to table, but I never told Nah.

It was not so much the act that bothered Nah but rather what he considered to be a purity of artistic intentions; that is, one should want to affectively share art rather than desiring money. Yet, forming such moralized desires was not an equitable option among all dancers. Tips on the beaches are an essential part of a dancer's income; this is very different than the ways in which money is exchanged at large luxury events and hotels where a tip bucket is never passed around. When I inquired about how tipping worked at the larger events, Anik explained that tipping was not at all expected because "artists never ask for tips." Dancers, however, made much more money at these events, and tips were not necessary. Thus, a spatial politics—beach shows versus luxury events—existed that intersected with age, ethnicity, and nationality.

Nah had worked hard to become accepted among island inhabitants and to be seen as what he termed an artist rather than a beach boy; indeed, he desired to remove the center from notions of beach labor and mostly pursued opportunities at elite resorts and hotels that were branded as luxury. Yet, because of their junior statuses, it was the Burmese dancers who performed the nightly shows at the party-style beach bar, while other dancers strictly did performances at the hotels, at private villas, and for weddings that were more lucrative and steeped in an upper-class acceptability. Dao explained, "At the luxury resorts, it's like a real show. We are trying to say something, you know? It's something different they [the audience] know is deeper. It's art."

The hotel and resort shows were also aesthetically different. The routines were highly choreographed and often practiced for days in advance. Dancers at the center had specific costumes, rather than casual beach-style attire, to perform in that resembled traditional Thai dress. The music, in turn, was not the DJ'd house music heard on the beaches but a mix of soft house and top 40 that had been pre-chosen with carefully choreographed moves. The private villas and re-sorts were exclusive venues, and sometimes dancers could also partake in a lav-ish buffet meal. Unlike the beach shows where dancers worked for many hours—performing multiple sets and then engaging with customers—the shows at resorts were approximately twenty-five minutes, and the pay was significantly more. These shorter sets meant that dancers did not breathe in toxic fumes for as long as beach dancers had to, and thus the physical toll on their bodies was significantly less. During fieldwork in 2016, I only went to one performance where Burmese dancers were performing at a luxury show. Nah and the other Thai dancers performed with them, and they practiced for two weeks leading up to the performance. In 2019, this had changed somewhat, as Nah's two most senior Burmese dancers, who had trained with him for years, also started doing the luxury shows when he was away; afterward, however, they were expected to go back to the beach bar and finish the evening shows there.

Nah also communicated that he worried about the lack of professionalism among some of the younger Burmese dancers, which he felt could ruin the rela-tionships he had built with managers at the luxury hotels. Indeed, moving fire dance from the beaches into the luxury resorts is a difficult task if you are not a *farang* performer because of the stigma surrounding the genre and overarching value structures of art in white neoliberal capitalist markets. Nah often spoke about how he was trying to teach the Burmese dancers to arrive on time, be re-spectful, and dress nicely. He often went to check in during their beach shows to "make sure they don't look like gangsters, like standing around and smoking cigarettes. They need to be polite also by way they look, so people will give them respect." Nah cared for the well-being of the Burmese dancers and often dis-cussed how he, too, had to learn to be an artist and had made many mistakes when he was young; he did not want them to repeat his mistakes. These politics of artistry emerged somewhat unintentionally and not necessarily solely because of ethnicity or nationality; it was also because of the ways in which age, economic

FIGURE 4.1.   Luxury show for a wedding, Koh Samui.

necessity, and resource scarcity intersect in this economy against a backdrop of Othering that all fire dancers face.

Anik also felt an allegiance to the Burmese dancers and was sympathetic to their plight. She wanted the center to offer a pathway to better employment and better pay, and indeed, their beach jobs were very well paid compared with others. Still, however, Anik felt their young ages meant they needed training to maintain a particular image of the fire art center. She was less concerned with monetary desires and more focused on managing their interactions with female tourists. She related that the center was initially open to any tourists who wanted to come and learn, and she would have the Burmese team advertise this at the beach bar each night. Anik felt, however, that this typically attracted women whom she characterized as "not serious." She described how the Burmese dancers brought tourist women whom they had met the night before and who would just sort of hang out with the guys but not be seriously interested in learning. She related,

> We spoke with the boys because they are the ones bringing the custom-
> ers. At the beginning, we were like now we have a nice place to wel-
> come tourists, so we started to give fliers out at the bar to advertise. I
> hadn't thought about all these girls and quickly we started to have girls
> coming here. But it was girls who didn't want to learn fire. They just
> wanted to come and watch, and to spend time with the fire spinners.
> So, at the beginning I was like, ok, we will see how it's going. And then

maybe six or eight months I ago, I was like, stop. I didn't want all these girls to be here. But we spoke with the students [Burmese dancers] and said, "Hey listen, this place here is not about that." They changed and they didn't bring any more of these kinds of girls.

This type of management also existed at the bar where they performed. The Thai boss of the beach bar where the Burmese team performed had also implemented a rule limiting their contact with tourist women. Anik explained, "The boss from Star Bar got really crazy like one year ago. You know the table they have that is only for firemen [fire dancers]? Every night there was about ten or twenty girls around this table dressed in super short skirts and everything and the boss said, 'I don't want any girls around this table.'" Indeed, I never saw female tourists at the small equipment table where the guys set up on the beach. I was, after some time, allowed to go in that area, but only after Nah spoke with the owner of the bar.

While Anik and Nah expressed their desires to help the Burmese dancers, not everyone at the center felt the same way. For Som, the competition the Burmese dancers brought to the islands, along with what he felt was a lack of artistry, was unacceptable. As we talked about advanced fire art tricks one day on the beach, Som related the following:

> SOM: You can ask the fire dancers here, "You know hybrid? You know isolation? You know anti-spin?" If they say they don't know, it means they are not in the *poi* yet. You just need to ask this question. Not many people know these tricks. You can ask the Burmese, "You know hybrid? No."
>
> AUTHOR: The students who study with Nah, how did they get to go there?
>
> SOM: Actually, before they worked in my friend's bar and their work was not so good because they thought they were cool. And then we kicked them out of the bar and none of them had a job because they had egos. With Burmese people, that's how I feel, you know? And they had nowhere to go, so Nah didn't have a choice, you know?

Som was not pleased that the Burmese students trained under Nah, particularly because they cut in on jobs and, as he saw it, devalued the art form. However, Som never spoke disparagingly about the Burmese while at the center, where I often saw him teaching the dancers from Myanmar, and even joking with them and chatting. Despite his personal feelings, at the center he shared.

These politics were not discussed by the Burmese dancers, who often spoke of how the center provided them with a lifeline not offered to other dancers from

Myanmar. Their beach jobs were better paid than most, and they were able to link in with a community that became like family for them. The Burmese dancers had a great amount of respect for Nah and their fellow Thai dancers, and they worked hard to fulfill the ideals upheld by Nah. Jes expressed,

> Here is like our home. We can do whatever we want, we can practice, it's very free. I really respect him [Nah] because he has a good heart. And he likes to give a chance to people. Nobody would teach Burmese people, but he did.

The center offered an important space for Thai and Burmese dancers to work together in the midst of industry-wide tensions and issues, but it was not a space devoid of politics. It was assumed that Thais were not in need of artistic mentoring, which created an internal structure reflecting geopolitical tensions and hierarchies in Thailand. Moreover, beach dancers were considered less artistic, creating a spatialized politics of belonging that structured resources and intersected with age, ethnicity, and nationality; this emerged each evening as the Burmese dancers went to the beaches and others (Thai and *farang* performers) went to exclusive resorts and villas. There was an understanding of the heightened survival needs of dancers from Myanmar, but there was also ambivalence about what Thai dancers felt were impure economic desires that risked devaluing the art form and the center's branding of Thai fire dance as a luxury art form.

The fire art center mirrors wider tensions surrounding livelihoods, mobilities, and global encounter on the islands. Burmese dancers are a somewhat ambivalent reminder of the precarity that all fire dancers face in the tourism industry. They are often younger and threaten the livelihoods and possibilities for social mobility of fire dancers in the first and second generations. These tensions map onto movement styles. The fast aesthetics that are characterized as being a Burmese style are a racialized bodily inscription that attempts to make visible those beach boys that can blend in, unknowingly, among Thai artists. While the center was a space designed to foster a sense of belonging and equity among all fire dancers, the Burmese dancers belonged differently and made less money.

The issues, however, do not preclude the sense of home and friendship that the center offered, which the Burmese dancers felt. Such dissonances are generative aspects of many communities and do not necessarily forestall solidarity and intimacy. As they shared together, the center dancers intervened in a neoliberal capitalist system that benefits from separation and competition over jobs; at the center, Thai and Burmese dancers shared time and resources in ways that generated feelings of belonging among dancers. However, Burmese dancers have vastly different experiences and types of precarity to contend with than do many of their Thai counterparts in the industry. Just as Thai dancers adopt different gendered surfaces (Van Esterik 2000) and moral imperatives to reimagine and ne-gotiate their lives and positionalities, so, too, do Burmese dancers. They employ fluid masculinities and construct morality in different, and sometimes compet-ing, ways. Burmese dancers define their moral worlds and foster affective con-nections that allow them to create communities on their own terms and in ways that attend to their particular migration histories and experiences.

Migrant Masculinities

> I took a van. Then hid in the forest. Many people go in big trucks and pay a lot of money. It's very dangerous, but they take many people because they will make more money that way. We have to go around the border and walk through the forest for five days just little by little. We had to crouch in the truck and then when we were at the border, we had to creep through the forest ten minutes at a time. So many Bur-mese people were killed like this, all packed in the truck. I feel lucky and I want to write a book about the travels of Burmese people. I have had an adventurous life. I was very scared when I did it, because I read about others who died. I was lucky. I was very worried because there are many police checks, so I was so happy when I first got here. Some people sell everything, get caught, and then cannot go back.

I share this story, told by Jes, as it is a common one among Burmese dancers and demonstrates the very different migration trajectories of Thais taking buses from villages to seek more income and those from Myanmar who cross the border in search of jobs and new opportunities while laden with debt and fears of being caught. The economic pressures loom large, as they often cannot easily return home and will face deportation, arrest, or worse. This precarity is different from that faced by Thai dancers, who, if they lose their jobs or do not make enough money, can easily return to their villages; Thai dancers also have the language skills, status, and connections to move around easily.

There is a pronounced focus among Thai dancers on delineating a moral fire artist as one who is not motivated by economic desires. However, dancers from Myanmar have very different economic and social pressures to contend with; money is part of survival and, as will be detailed below, also considered moral and affective. For Burmese dancers, beach labor and desires for money held different meanings and were an essential component in creating and reimagining gendered moralities and the affective social bonds that connected them with others.

Research on migration has demonstrated the fluidity of gender as particular ideals are maintained, contested, and reimagined across spaces (Datta et al.

FIGURE 4.2. Fire dancer, Koh Samui.

2009). Migrant men might employ a "flexible and strategic masculinity" through which they withhold aspects of their gendered selves that might be valued in their home countries (Batnitzky et al. 2009, 1280). Others shift fluidly among different masculinities in particular spaces; Steven C. McKay (2007) found that Filipino seamen performed an "exemplary masculinity" when in the Philippines despite having subordinate masculinities while at sea because of their racial and class positionings. The industry constructed a subordinate masculinity to keep Filipinos cheap and tractable, much like the Burmese fire dancers, yet the seamen forged their own subjectivities that contested these positionings. The Burmese dancers at the center actualized an array of gendered surfaces that Nah upheld as moral—particularly in crafting an artist masculinity that was professional and motivated by affective sharing. The Burmese dancers were also Theravada Buddhists, and moralities surrounding the elaboration kin economies resonated easily. However, outside of the center, they had different perceptions and surfaces that related to masculine ideals in Myanmar.

Ward Keeler asserts that masculinities in Myanmar are formed in the tension between the idealized figure of the Buddhist monk and the productive male. He states, "Burman notions of an idealized masculinity falls, ironically, on both sides of Connell's hegemonic masculinity. In the dual images of an active, assertive, sexually athletic and productive male, on the one hand, and a remote and sexually ascetic monk, on the other, we find two apparently radically different representations of idealized masculinity" (2017, 228). Hegemonic masculinity is a negotiation between being able to enact power through hierarchical relations with others—through money and sex—and complete autonomy from attachments, represented by the ascetic monk.[1] The flexible ways in which masculinities are made in negotiation with such figures, as well as through migration, are in line with the logic of gendered surfaces that is centered in contextually based transformative possibilities (Van Esterik 2000).

The gendered moralities of fire dancers oscillate around these ideals in highly spatialized ways. While at the center, Nah was promoting ideals of detachment—from money, from ego, from women—and encouraged intensive bodily training and self-discipline that referenced the figure of the monk. At the center, Burmese dancers shaped their surfaces around such ideals—often describing how they had learned to feel art in a different way as their desires for money decreased. On the beaches, however, the dancers from Myanmar had different perspectives about the intersections of fire dance, gender, and morality. They used the times on the beach to reinterpret and reimagine particular moralities, motivations, and the deviancy ascribed to them by Thai dancers.

Affinitive Labor

During my time at the fire art center in 2016, I wondered whether the Burmese dancers were showcasing a moral artistic gendered surface they believed Nah wanted out of an allegiance to him and the center. While they belonged differently, I sensed that they were appreciative of Nah and felt lucky to have found such a community. And they often expressed this, even when Nah was not around. I worked hard to carve out time alone with the Burmese dancers, but Nah was frequently present at the center and their intensive jobs meant that there were few opportunities. I returned to Koh Samui in 2019 when Nah and Anik were away, and I spent each day and night with the Burmese dancers. I noticed that the dancers did not go to the center every day anymore but instead would choose particular days to get together under the leadership of Jes, Nah's most advanced Burmese student, who led the team. Most days, instead of going to the center, they would head to the beach bar early to practice, share conversation, and warm up. I started spending more and more time on the beach with them before their shows. This was a time when they expressed perspectives on some of the moralities and affective connections they felt were important motivators in their lives as fire dancers.

I would arrive at the bar just as the sun was going down. I walked past tourists on loungers smoking shisha, drinking cocktails, and eating food. I would head toward the back area where the Burmese team prepared for the show and hung out. The sounds were quite different if you listened past the English pop music and tourist chatter at the bar—Burmese phrases filled the soundscape as many beach laborers gathered informally during short breaks from work. In the shadows at the edges of the tourist areas, the dancers would wrap their fire staffs with new cotton to the sounds of Burmese hip-hop played from someone's phone. They would chat with each other in Burmese, and my position as an outsider would be prominently marked, as I cannot understand Burmese. This was a time carved out for them. Chats were interspersed with bits of laughter and smiles, and I would quietly sit and share time with them. A few of the dancers were experts with photography, and they would sometimes help me prepare the camera for the evening so that we could get photos to advertise their shows and post on social media.

After preparing their equipment, they would make their way toward the beach, dropping their toys and kerosene in the sand next to the table where they coalesced during the performance. They worked together to carve out a space in the sand to dance. Burmese workers from other beach bars would stop by and shake hands as glances, small smiles, and waves were exchanged from afar with others who were serving, selling trinkets, and giving henna tattoos and pineapples to tourists. Often, a server would come over and try one dancer's toys, and others would join in to show him a move. These were small acts of sharing that emerged in tiny windows of breaks from work, opportunities that have facilitated almost all of these young men's transitions from jobs in construction and restaurants to fire dancing. In the short times before performances, the dancers provided similar opportunities to their friends who wished to become dancers. Sometimes they would gather around someone's phone to watch YouTube videos of particular moves they wanted to learn and spend time practicing with each other. Eventually, Jes would determine that it was time for the show to begin. In 2019, the dancers started wearing masks during the performances, which they felt added an artistic theatrical element to their shows. I wondered, however, if it also provided anonymity for dancers who did not have legal paperwork. Inspired by the American hip-hop dance crew the Jabbawockeez, the

Burmese dancers put their masks on and prepared themselves along the beach in a line, and Jes would blow a whistle to get the crowd's attention. During the show, the small table where they would sit and wait to dance would be surrounded with other friends from Myanmar who were taking a break from work; they would come to talk and watch the show, which seemed to transform a time and place of touristic labor into one that involved the creation and maintenance of a community.

I often marked these informal moments as important, although I was not initially sure why. Reading back over my fieldnotes, they emerged from the pages as contexts carved out specifically for Burmese people, as small opportunities for community-making on their own terms and in the midst of labor. Each evening, the Burmese dancers did not simply go to work but actualized forms of conviviality among the many people who worked on the beach. Dai Kojima's (2016) conception of "affinitive labor" captures these dynamics. In his research with queer male migrant Japanese men, Kojima found that practices of care and community were actualized through labor and entrepreneurial endeavors. These affinitive labors created valuable kinships for people navigating wider exclusionary structures. Among fire dancers, their quotidian labor—which takes place behind the scenes of performance—generates affective social bonds for young Burmese men in the tourism industry. Their beach labor and immersion in the rhythms of neoliberal capitalism provided the setting for communities of belonging to be built.

Unlike how market exchange and the tourism industry are positioned as corruptive of such forms of conviviality, among Burmese dancers on the beaches, they facilitated such affective connections. The beach was a key meeting place for young Burmese men who often arrived on the islands alone. Many told of how they would arrive and meet another Burmese person on the beach who helped them gain employment, housing, and friends. These connections were essential, as their undocumented status meant that they could not go around and inquire about work; they needed someone to help them into the industry. Myint, who had danced with the center team since 2016, shared, "We all came here alone and didn't know anybody, and we came to look for work. We would walk around and try to find others from Myanmar and see if their boss will take someone without a passport." Jes agreed and explained his story: "I came here, and I had no friends. I was alone. But fortunately, I met a friend of mine just on the road. I stopped him and he took me to his home and I stayed there, and we went to find a job at the restaurant on the beach."

Jes's journey from his home in Myiek, in the south of Myanmar, described previously, happened when he was a teenager. His family was very poor, and knowing others who had made this journey across the Thai border successfully,

FIGURE 4.3.   Fire dancer, Koh Samui.

he found a broker, took what money he and his family had raised, and left. Jes found himself initially in a small border town, unable to speak Thai, working at a pharmacy, a job that the broker had arranged. With a dream to learn English, he decided to move to a tourist area and hopped on a bus and then took a ferry to Koh Samui. He arrived on the island alone and walked along the beach road filled with tourists, restaurants, and shops—an area where many Burmese people work—wondering how he might approach a shop owner and carefully ask for work without legal documents. Through his lucky encounter with his friend who happened to pass by, he was able to get a job as a server at a beach restaurant. He faced intense language barriers at first, but the beach offered a place of connection and solace because there were people he could speak Burmese with. He explained that almost all Burmese people knew each other on the island and that "for us, if I know one person and he has friends, we will speak Burmese together, so it's easy to get to know each other."

Being on the beaches is what facilitated an entry into a fire dance. This is a job that is better paid, is safer, and comes with more freedom, as there is less surveillance by Thai bosses than with jobs serving or in construction. Jes worked as a waiter at a beach restaurant for some time, and there was a fire show at the adjacent bar. After discovering that fire dancers made more money than servers and had fewer working hours, he decided to learn fire dancing. Like many other

Burmese dancers, Jes learned on the sidelines with Burmese friends in short breaks during his shift and through YouTube videos. Jes eventually met Zaw, who danced at the bar next door and was among the first Burmese dancers in Thailand. Zaw taught Jes as much as possible in a short period of time and helped him into the scene. Jes was thrust into what he called "the fire dance life" one night when a Thai dancer did not show up for his shift. Jes remembered being on stage shaking, barely able to spin, but he knew it was an opportunity he had to seize; he was asked to join that team, and Zaw later introduced Jes to Nah.

These types of chance meetings and opportunities are a common way people become dancers, and many go on to teach others, resulting in thick social networks along the beaches. Tun, who was from Kawthuang, arrived when he was twelve, and he discussed how he started to recruit young Burmese people into the fire dance industry. He stated, "At that time, they [fire dancers] were almost all Thais. I would teach on the beaches. They usually have to start dancing for no pay, but if a Thai dancer was away, I would beg my boss to let my friend perform." Bringing people into a team often resulted in a Thai dancer losing their job, which has likely fueled the tensions in the scene and cast Burmese dancers as not real fire artists because they are motivated by economic greed.

Their methods of learning are done quickly in small breaks and moments, as dancers try to help each other into better jobs. Many, when they first join a team, do not have the highly honed skills developed through years of practice, which is visible when they perform on stage for the first time. Yet, despite how their participation is framed by Thai dancers as not centered in sharing and community, they view their own learning as immersed in relationships among Burmese people, specifically. While they are positioned as the harbingers of competition fueled by desires for *farang* women and greed, the dancers from Myanmar are integrated into tightly woven tapestries of support. Burmese dancers viewed these pursuits as acts of support and survival that ushered young men into more livable, hopeful, and safe lives. Through his job as a dancer, for instance, Jes was able to save enough money to enroll in a university where he studied philosophy. He also learned to read, speak, and write both Thai and English. Now, Jes is a key person on the island who helps others who are newly arrived to secure jobs and connect with other Burmese people. These dancers, like their Thai counterparts, also learn as part of communities of sharing, although theirs are formed in impromptu moments along the beaches and in spaces between work rather than those more formally organized such as at the center. The beach facilitated a space for sharing and the creation of communities of care among young men who helped each other toward better lives in small moments during their labor.

The Affective Materiality of Money

While many Thai fire dancers' conceptions of morality were centered around developing noneconomic desires, transnational migration often creates an enhanced relationship with money as it becomes "a detachable form of masculine potency and a means of exerting agency at a distance" (Osella and Osella 2000, 128). This potency, however, gets reinterpreted as capital is transferred through local economies and moralities (Osella and Osella 2000). As we see with Thai and Burmese dancers moving away from their home villages, there is a complicated linkage between money, morality, and gender as dancers seek to earn an income through dance while aligning with Theravada Buddhist–informed ideals that decry material attachments. The center in this way functioned as a space that cleansed money, moving it from payment to donations, and from work to art. The moralities Burmese dancers expressed on the beaches, however, did not revolve around the same ideals as Nah's but directly involved their ability to earn money so they could assert themselves as independent men—the "productive male" that Keeler speaks of (2017).

Stretching his arms out along the beach one day Myint stated, "This is my home. It's so easy here. Even if I don't play fire here, I can find another job. Everything here is good—the money and my life." Financial security was something each dancer I spoke with communicated as important to their sense of belonging and ease on the island. Indeed, Myint had met so many people through fire dancing that fears of losing his job did not bother him. Dancers' earning abilities, in turn, also linked with how they upheld their moral duties with their families in Myanmar. Jes explained, "I am happy because I can send money back home. So, my parents are happy." Many dancers referenced how their families longed for them to be closer, but the lack of jobs and low salaries in Myanmar meant that they would not make enough to support their families in ways they deemed important. Thar said, "I stayed in Thailand because if go back to Burma I will want to stay, like if I see my parents. But there are no jobs there, so I cannot live there." I asked about how his parents felt about his job as a fire dancer, and he related, "When I was young, they didn't like it, but now they think it is ok because I take care of myself." While the Thai dancers attempted to construct their desires as not tied to gaining money and saw it as antithetical to affective connections, the Burmese dancers were adamant that their desires to dance were centered in access to economic resources, as this access facilitated such connections.

One day as Jes and I chatted privately at the center, when Nah was not present, he discussed how this desire fueled him to learn about people in ways that generated tips. He explained,

For me, when I am playing fire, I love to watch the customers and look into their eyes—do they like it or not? You can learn one thing from customers and that is, you are going to know how to control people, how to attract people to you. So, you are going to know about people, how to read people's minds.

AUTHOR: How do you do that? While playing are you looking at them?
JES: Ya. Because after playing fire I go into the audience to get some tips. So, I do this every day and lately I watch and think about it: Who loves our show? Who didn't watch? And I can read their minds, too. I read a lot of books about people, about how to read people's minds. So, I think it's great because I only watch their eyes and I know what they want.

Jes had invested time in learning techniques to properly assess the audience before he went around with the tip bucket. At very large bars, such as the one that he performed at, dancers must be strategic about whom they approach for tips as it is not possible to go to each person. Making money thus was not simply a benefit to sharing an aesthetic experience and practicing self-discipline and detachment; it was a main motivator in performance for Jes and others on his team. This is not to say that their discussions of how they learned to develop a love for fire art under Nah's tutelage, as Jes expressed in chapter 3, were not genuine. Rather, they oscillated around these different gendered ideals—detachment from material items and the autonomy and power that money provided.

Moreover, a politics surrounding socioeconomic status means not all had the ability to foster such detached motivations and center their practice in aesthetic pleasure; the stakes of not receiving tips is much higher for those who make less and cannot easily change jobs. Indeed, on my last day on the island in 2019, I asked Jes what he thought was the most important thing he wanted people to know about fire dance, and he expressed, "We meet European guys who do this, and they do fire art for travel and like living this life. They come here and ask to work for tips and sort of live like that. But for us it's not the same. They search for happiness, but for us it's about survival. I need money to send home." While he was referring specifically to *farang* dancers who came to the center to share but also wanted to make money while they were on holiday, his point reflects the politics at the center—well-paid Thai dancers may not always have the same economic and legal pressures as those dancers from Myanmar.

The dancers from Myanmar reimagined the moralities of the fire art center on the beaches and viewed making money and the pursuit of high-paying jobs as moral. Making money not only provided opportunities to actualize power and autonomy but also provided the material means to sustain kin economies with their families in Myanmar. Unlike their Thai colleagues, this economic desire was, for them, moral in that money sustained transnational emotional connections, while their pursuit of it also generated the affinitive labor that built communities on the beaches (Kojima 2016). Money, in this sense, did not disrupt affective connections but actually forged them among laborers and between young men and their families in Myanmar. Burmese dancers did not attempt to cast themselves as moral men in the same ways that Thai dancers did, particularly when they were outside the center space. Rather, they embodied morality *through* economic exchange.

The figure of the monk and Nah's centering of detachment and self-discipline were never erased. Jes, for instance, sometimes highlighted what he learned from Nah to position himself as different from other Burmese dancers. As we chatted about the Burmese team, he expressed, "For most of them, it's just a good job, not like art, but it gives them time, freedom. If I got another job, I would still play. I learned from Nah and he feels it, but others might not." While Jes used the same discourse of fire dance being more than a job for him, he referenced another important reason why many Burmese migrants want to dance: fire dancing allowed them the freedom to create connections with others.

Freedom

Phyo, who was in his early twenties, stated, "It's a good job because it gives us time. We love fire dance because we are doing our own job. It's not like working at a restaurant where the boss pushes us even when there are no customers. It's [fire art] our own job." All of the Burmese dancers I met started out in service or construction industries, which they related were dangerous, and with long hours and intense surveillance by bosses. The dancers expressed that the increased independence and autonomy offered through fire dance allowed them to make not only more money but also more connections with people. Soe explained, "At first in the restaurant, I was not happy to go to work and I cannot talk to people or anything. But now it is not boring, and I can talk with people. I feel good." Being able to actualize connections and conversations also linked into what they felt was a different lifestyle that the beaches supported. Jes's friend who worked next to the bar shared that he initially went back to Myanmar but returned to Thailand again and related, "I want to go back but then I will be back here again because there are no jobs, and the salary is so low. Everybody wants to go home but it is a different style of living there." Many of the dancers, even though they were paid less than Thais, were able to travel and participate in the cosmopolitan culture of the beach in ways that would not otherwise be possible. Jes agreed: "I don't want to be a waiter again. With fire dance, you can play and talk to customers. It's more free. The living style is free. You can do what you want and learn everything."

The informality on the beaches, where dancers engage with tourists and other laborers, allows for multiple relations to take shape. Indeed, those who worked in other jobs and came by to visit had very short breaks. While fire dancers performed and technically worked long hours, there was much less surveillance, and part of their labor revolved around engaging with tourists directly as they mingled after the shows. Having the freedom to form friendships and learn from tourists was consistently cited as something that made them feel an attachment to the beach and their lives on the island. Burmese fire dancers have learned multiple languages from tourists and have acquired a variety of different skills. In turn, they have friends all over the world whom they stay in touch with through social media. By engaging with tourists, they experiment with gender in a transnational context that is valuable and desirable to them.

Fire dancing on the beaches, however, is not without risk, and their newfound freedom came with other forms of precarity and danger. While most spectators might consider getting burned as the most prominent risk, it is the unseen damage done to the lungs that is the greatest concern among dancers. While those who dance at luxury resorts and parties need only perform a few nights a week or month for short, twenty-minute sets, the beach dancers from Myanmar dance every night for hours. In 2019, I sensed Jes was seriously contemplating leaving the industry for this reason. He explained, "Fire dance is a better job because it has more freedom, but it has risk. There is much more risk on the lungs. All of us have black in our nose after the show." As I came to learn, many of the older dancers from Myanmar were also struggling. Myint said that he felt the industry was becoming even more saturated and now there was competition *among* Burmese dancers: "Now there are so many dancers. Even since the last time you came [2016]. Now bars are hiring dancers for very cheap. Maybe before it was 10,000 baht a night and tips [for a team], and now some teams will play for only 3,000 baht. Now I want to be a DJ and learn about DJing." Myint had recently started dating at a Chinese tour guide who had moved to the island to help set up tours for the large influx of Chinese tourists. He had begun learning Mandarin and was helping with the tours as he made his exit plan. Jes, as well, noted about this job, "I want something even more my own," and I understood this as a reference to how his freedom and autonomy are somewhat limited, as he is positioned as subordinate and under the control of Nah. Jes started learning photography and had set up an informal school to teach other Burmese people English and Thai.

Both Jes and Myint, however, have found possible pathways to leave the industry because of the connections they have made on the beaches and through fire dancing. What is clear is that communities of belonging form through the labor on the beaches as young men teach, learn, and support each other toward better lives in small moments during breaks and in the midst of their jobs. Through their labor, the beach was not experienced as a place of immorality, unruly sexuality, and marginalization that permeates the narratives throughout this book; rather, the beach was a site of freedom and connection through which they rewrote moral scripts, life pathways, and gendered ideals. Among the Burmese dancers, the beaches become sites of belonging through their labor and immersion in tourist market economies.

Fire dance is a site of care and belonging among migrant men, as well as a platform for the mediation of local and transnational gendered moral ideals. As Thai dancers attempt to sustain their participation in the industry amid the influx of cheaper laborers, boundaries of belonging are created that exclude dancers from Myanmar through highlighting their perceived deficiencies as moral and mature men. The discussions and differences between the fire art center and the beach highlight how masculinity for Burmese young men is implicated in one's ability to be autonomous and not controlled by others. Yet, this desire was also in dialogue with the affective attachments they had to their mentor, Nah. The center sought to create a community of belonging among Thai and Burmese dancers, as Nah taught the Burmese dancers how to achieve an artist masculinity that indexed Theravada Buddhist–informed ideals of unattachment and self-discipline. The Burmese dancers were flexible in their adoption of these principles at the center, while on the beaches they actualized income-earning gendered moralities to showcase their independence and maturity. These different fluid masculinities can also be thought of as enactments based on the principle of *kalatesa*—that is, a careful attentiveness to context in one's shifting of gendered surfaces (Van Esterik 2000).

As they reimagined the deviancy ascribed to their bodies and labor, Thai dancers often positioned dancers from Myanmar as deviant beach boys who were motivated by material desires and did not learn through sharing in a community; this manifested on their bodies through the aesthetic of fast spinning. Fast spinning, which often appears when someone is nervous and tense and does not know quite what to do, is also the embodiment of a chance opportunity to seize the moment and being able to pivot quickly to access jobs that have more earning potential and freedom. The moral ideals of Thai dancers were not always possible or valued by dancers from Myanmar who faced different, and often intensified, forms of precarity that meant dependence on material attachments for their survival. The pursuit of money, in turn, actualized affective connections that provided a sense of belonging on the beaches and in the transnational networks of support they engaged in with their families. Morality was lived on the beaches not through the structures that limited desires centered in economic success but through building relations that often involved the pursuit of and exchange of money. For the Burmese dancers who worked at the center, money and the beaches were not corrupting forces that were antithetical to moral principles and affective connections; rather, they were intimately intertwined with them. The labor of fire dance cemented these men in affinities that made the beach and the island a place where they belonged despite the social narratives that positioned them otherwise.

THE EVERYDAY COMFORT OF PRACTICE

**I have many talents, and that's what makes people go, "Wow!"
That's how you get respect—because of the talent. You see all
those toys? Maybe someone will come and try them and do many
tricks, and you will think that they are amazing. They have talent,
and people respect that.**

—Som

Out of all of the dancers I met, Som could perform with the most toys—*poi*, sticks, rope dart, fans, double staff, fire juggling—and was very skilled at all of them. His set of extensive talents, as he called them, were developed through an insatiable desire to learn and to practice new skills. Som and I were sitting on loungers outside a guesthouse owned by his friend's mother on Koh Samui's Chaweng Beach one day when he explained the connection between respect and talent. He elaborated on his skills while pointing toward the large array of his toys—*poi*, ropes, chains, juggling pins—that were scattered across a section of the beach.

Most days, Som would come to the beach to practice. He would pick up a toy, play for a while, and then wander in the sand, smiling at tourists. Interspersed throughout his daily beach practice were breaks during which he would sit in a lounger and watch YouTube videos and then walk over to converse with his friend at the guesthouse. Som and his toys took up space on the beach in way that was slightly out of time and place, drawing attention from passersby. The daytime was mostly reserved for tourists who would swim, sunbathe, and casually walk in the sand. Som claimed this section of beach as his own and spent time practicing and honing his various talents while enjoying the daytime heat.

Som's beachside days illuminate the "ordinary affects" of island life—"a shifting assemblage of practices and practical knowledges, a scene of both liveness and exhaustion, a dream of escape or of the simple life. Ordinary affects are the varied, surging capacities to affect and to be affected that give everyday life the quality of a continual motion of relations, scenes, contingencies, and emergences" (Stewart 2007, 1–2). Som's days on the beach formed part of the atmospheric intensities of island tourism life that pulled, pushed, and seduced him into particular rhythms, assemblages, and worldings (Little 2012). I first understood Som's everyday affects as a constellation of contentment and a casual, comfortable impetus to practice and learn new hobbies, enjoy the sun, and take it easy—what Thais might refer to as being *sabai sabai* (content). Yet, various energies underpinned Som's motivations and influenced the life pathways he pursued. His laidback practice of talents was supported by a flurry of affects through which Som negotiated life in tourist economies and his dreams for the extraordinary.

Sabai Sabai on Koh Samui

The lives of inhabitants on the tourist islands are determined by different cycles than the 9:00 a.m. to 5:00 p.m. pattern my body functioned on, which continued to rouse me at 6:30 a.m. each morning throughout fieldwork. Island time is clocked by the intensity of the heat, which means that early evening feels somewhat like a morning; it is a time of hustle and bustle as people get ready for night markets and sharing food, walking, and gathering outdoors. Late afternoon is more akin to a beginning rather than what I am used to in Canada, where I sense it as a close to the day. Larger patterns and cycles create ebbs and flows of tourists, work, and income that impact the overall vibe on the islands: the low season, typically from July to October, is ushered in through hotter weather and the monsoon season, which means fewer tourists are in Thailand. The moon cycles, in turn, set rhythmic patterns of tourist arrivals and departures across the islands; young backpackers flock to Koh Phangan for the Full Moon Parties, moving from other islands, and then flowing back again to Koh Samui, to Koh Tao, and even to Koh Phi Phi on the Andaman coast after the monthly Full Moon Party finishes. These interconnected and layered cycles structure how time feels and how life is lived. High season brings in numerous tourists, and an abundance of resources with a more exuberant feel—inhabitants have money and life is lived more easily because there is a sense of economic security. Low season, with its slowed influx of tourist dollars, means that scarcity is more presently felt, and anxiety haunts the edges of contentment. Even the most abundant and happy months, however, have an underlying ambivalence that livelihoods depend on tourist money at all. Scarcity always lurks, often expressing itself through inhabitants' discussions of a slowing industry and the quiet takeover of local businesses by large corporations and elite.

This veiled scarcity manifests itself in other ways, as well, and none clearer to me than the bulldozed field halfway down the Chaweng strip, close to where Som would practice on the beach in 2016. The empty space was all that was left of my favorite restaurant, Mama's, which used to stand proudly as one of few family-owned businesses left on the Chaweng strip. Each evening Mama's restaurant was packed with people eager for her family to prepare food that tasted like Thai food, and not the watered-down versions served at the multiple large establishments that were taking over the area. These monstrous restaurants all had different names, but each had the exact same menus and prices and primarily employed Burmese people as servers and cooks. Carefully disguised chain establishments, they drew in tourists through appearing as independent local entities. On the afternoon when Mama's was destroyed, I saw the Thai military removing people and belongings. I rushed back to the guesthouse where I stayed to ask what was happening and received a careful answer—*mai pen rai* (don't worry, never mind); the army was reclaiming land that did not actually belong to Mama and her family, I was told. Three years later, I returned to this same spot to see three more of the chain restaurants filling the field. Mama's business was gone in the flash of day, with the open field left to remind inhabitants that even in times of abundance, paucity can pounce from unexpected places; island life is not *sabai sabai* for all.

Sabai sabai was among the first phrases I learned when I moved to Bangkok in 2010. It is a seductive cultural idiom for tourists and expats. The expression is easily found through a Google search and is presented as a key phrase for tourists to know. *Sabai* translates as content, relaxed, or comfortable, and generally describes a state of well-being. It is also used to ask someone how they are doing when greeting: *sabai dee mai?* One might answer with *sabai dee* to express contentment. Repeating the word twice—*sabai sabai*—expresses an added emphasis on such comfortable feelings. If one is fully relaxed, enjoying time with a worry-free sensibility, with no pressing matters, one might feel *sabai sabai*. The phrase is ubiquitous in the tourism industry; it is the name of guesthouses, massage parlors, and restaurants, and it is printed across t-shirts and knick-knacks in tourist markets. *Sabai sabai* is also tattooed on *farang* bodies as a permanent attachment to the particular affects Thailand sells. These idioms engage tourists' desires for the slow relaxation of a worry-free vacation while producing a potent and felt perception of exotic cultural difference that is part of Thailand's allure.

When I first arrived in Thailand, I was told by other *farangs* of how the Thais on the islands were the epitome of *sabai sabai* and could be seen lazing in hammocks for most the day, sentiments that are echoed in tourist blogs and books. However, the affective sense of comfort and relaxation is not equally experienced; what might appear as a *sabai sabai* life is supported by a whirlwind of activity. A hustle is necessitated by tourist economies that structure how money ebbs and flows and the rhythms of neoliberal capitalism that underpin the textures of island life. While tourists' experiences of islands may create a feeling of slowing down, a time of relaxation and long, unfolding sunny days, it feels much different over long periods of time. The longer I spent living on the islands, the more I began to feel the rhythms of the everyday as intensely fast and busy; old establishments were torn down, new bars were built in days, trees were cut for more land, boats came in and out carrying hundreds of tourists upward of ten times a day, piers filled with impatient people searching for their luggage, taxis rushed to get people to their booked tours, and cleaners hustled to remake rooms for new arrivals—all so tourists can feel *sabai sabai*.

These different temporalities, rhythms, and labor epitomize how "some bodies can 'have' comfort, only as an effect of the work of others, where the work itself is concealed from view" (Ahmed, 2004, 149). Feeling comfortable, as Sara Ahmed argues, is an embodied process centered in encounters between bodies and spaces. She argues that "comfort is the effect of bodies being able to 'sink' into spaces that have already taken their shape. Discomfort is not simply a choice or decision . . . but an effect of bodies inhabiting spaces that do not take or 'extend' their shape" (2004, 152). Not all bodies feel comfort in the same ways, and tourism sites are set up to take the shape of tourist bodies. However, Som took time on the beach—day-by-day—creating and shaping that space to his body and his own personal pursuits of comfort and contentment.

For Som, carving out comfort on Koh Samui was necessitated on having the freedom to spend his days on the beach practicing and learning new talents. Som's days and cycles of time were different than most dancers and laborers on the islands. Like me, he rose early. Som only danced a few nights a month, which meant that he was out and about early to start his day. He was part of Nah's team, discussed in chapter 3, but he insisted he was only participating to pay back a favor to Nah for mentoring him. Som's main source of income came from traveling to Koh Phangan to perform at the large beach parties—Full, Half, and Black Moon Parties—with a different team of dancers. Som was very much on the move, and his travels were motivated by the same moon cycles that the tourists moved with. While his home base was on Koh Samui, he was often away performing, and his days included hopping on buses, trains, and ferries to Bangkok and Koh Phangan and other islands.

Som loved to travel, and these trips brought cherished sparks of spontaneity to everyday life on Koh Samui. Being in control of his work and schedule was something he was proud of. He stated, "I have enough. I only work six days a month. I get 30,000 baht. It's enough, you know? The rest of the time, I sleep and practice. I don't work every day. That's how I respect myself. The artist's life is not easy. I practice eight hours a day. I need to practice. But I work for myself. If you work for yourself, you are cool. You get respect. If you work in a factory, who can respect you?" Som shared these sentiments after speaking about the influx of Burmese dancers who he believed were taking jobs away from Thais. But Som had enough (*pho phiang*), he explained, which was considered in terms of enough to eat, enough to pay for rent and gas, and some money for fun. Most importantly, Som had the freedom to manage his days and most evenings as he pleased. That his schedule did not align with the typical rhythms of fire dancers—six days per week, 7:00 p.m. to 2:00 a.m.—provided respect that Som felt outweighed the amount of money one had. Having enough—money and time—created a sense of comfort in Som's life, or at least it appeared to.

Som rented an apartment close to the airport, far away from the tourist strip, and around noon he would ride his *motocy* down to Chaweng Beach to begin his day of practicing talents. While I hung out with Som at the fire art center as part of Nah's team, for our one-on-one conversations, he preferred to meet at his practice spot. I would walk the forty minutes down the Chaweng tourist strip through a sensory overload that I came to appreciate over time: smells of garbage and strangely seasoned popular "Thai" dishes with not quite the right ingredients, fuel from cars, and smoky scents from the small roadside barbeques cooking chicken and pork skewers; sounds of repetitive "Hello, how are you?" from people hired to coax tourists into the restaurants, a barrage of beeping horns from taxis, and the roars of *motocys*—an atmosphere that keeps the senses on high alert. I would arrive at the small laneway that twists and curves around a series of guesthouses toward the beach. I loved the moment turning the corner to go down the path to the guesthouse when the sensory experience changed dramatically: my nose would fill with salt water and the flowery scents from the trees that lined the beaches. The sounds would mellow and the cluttered noise from the strip faded away. Walking across the sand, I would look for Som's toys on the beach to see if he was there and sit in a beach lounger watching him practice. He would eventually take a break and come strolling over casually, looking almost tourist-like in his board shorts and flip flops, his long beach-like hair styled by wind and salt water.

Each day that Som practiced and learned on this stretch of beach, tourists looked on—he moved from practicing flow art with various toys, to learning new songs on the guitar, to creating balloon art, to breakdancing in the sand. His set of talents initially appeared to me as a few too many disjointed hobbies strewn about the beach. His friend at the guesthouse agreed and would laughingly point toward Som's toys and say, "*tingtong* Som" (eccentric, odd). Som honed his skills vigorously and to dizzying effects for those of us who stood at the edges watching and listening as he explained and experimented with a new interest each week. It seemed as if every time we met, Som was practicing something new that he had learned from a tourist friend or through YouTube videos: new languages, sewing, the powers of crystals, Thai massage. His talents extended well beyond flow art and encompassed such things as playing guitar, DJing, break dancing, performing magic tricks, and clowning, to name only a few of the skills Som acquired. In 2016, he also started to build the equipment used in fire dancing to sell to other dancers and tourists. His daily rhythms were decidedly different; they were determined by his own needs, and in particular his desire to spend his days practicing, learning, and honing talents.

A charismatic character, Som engaged passersby in conversation when they looked over at what he was doing. He might smile at someone and tell a quick joke or show them a card trick, something Som had done since he started in the tourist industry years before. Som referred to this daily activity as "the study life," which he pursued through watching tutorials on YouTube, through learning from new friends and acquaintances he met in the industry and along the stretch of beach, and through his own experimentation. He regaled me with tales of people whom he met who taught him different talents: DJs in Phuket, a Portuguese juggler on Bangkok's Khao San Road where he worked once selling shoes, taxi drivers who showed him magic tricks, break-dancers at beach parties, and the French and Japanese *poi* spinners in Santichaiprakhan Park whom he still played with. Som's multifaceted abilities, as well as the histories and friendships that created them, were displayed for all to see on the beach—*poi*, staffs, ropes, juggling balls, guitars, and clown costumes. They took up a significant amount of space in an area marked mostly for tourists, a space that Som made his own with a sizable conglomeration of talents that demanded respect or, at the very least, appreciative notice. Som made this space comfortable in how he crafted it to suit his needs and body (Ahmed 2004).

Som embodied what I initially viewed as a *sabai sabai* approach to life that his free schedule allowed for—days spent nonchalantly practicing toys, chatting with people, and hanging around the beach learning new things. Som's practice and acquisition of hobbies gave the appearance of someone living in the content abundance of high season at all times of year. Yet it was not so much gaining respect or being able to lead life outside of normative work routines, necessarily, that were the ultimate motivators; underneath the surface of contentment were feelings of security and possibility that this quotidian practice of gaining hobbies offered. Som's *sabai sabai* days spent on the section of tourist beach generated a dissonant comfort through which contentment and concern danced together in continuous friction to produce new worldings and dreams.

Som explained, "There are many things to learn in life. Everybody has a different dream, a different lifestyle, and a different way to live their life. My world is the entertainment life, like the nightlife. But the nightlife can be useful for the day life, like for learning how to live and how to survive." Som grabbed my small notebook and pen to explain. He began drawing separate circles with words representing each of his hobbies in the middle. Each circle was then carefully connected with a line to the largest circle in the middle of the paper, where he wrote the word "entertainer." The resultant drawing was many separate circles of skills connected together through the entertainer in the middle. As he completed the drawing, Som explained that an entertainer can "connect all the arts": "I am not good at everything, but I know how to connect it all. If you are an entertainer, you know it all, like how to control everybody. If you are an entertainer, it means you can perform fire, light shows, and DJing at the same time. You are the main artist. I want to be the main artist." At the heart of the assemblage of talents drawn on the notepad was Som, the entertainer, who was able to link together what appeared as a jumbled set of activities and spin out these various talents into something more. Som was not only practicing sets of skills but also developing himself as a person who is able to shift and move through multiple skills sets, a person who is independent and self-reliant.

Som had strong views on how desires for money needed to be separated from artistic pursuits, as such desires could cloud an artist's ability to share with others and affect audiences, as discussed in previous chapters. Yet the comforts that money could bring influenced Som's pursuit of talents and his goal of being an entertainer. In all respects, Som had overcome the poverty of his early years in the Northeast and the financial struggles he faced when he first began working in the tourism industry; Som recounted how he used to sleep on the beaches because he could not afford a place to stay, referring to these nights as when he stayed in a 1,000-star hotel. Yet anxieties about the security of livelihoods on the islands haunted the conversations I had with him. It became clear that practicing and honing talents were about more than a relaxed pursuit and *sabai sabai* days on the beaches—it was, for Som, also about economic survival in increasingly harsh and volatile tourism industries in which one's position as a dancer was never guaranteed past the next gig.

Desires for economic security also influenced the vision of the entertainer that Som actualized each day on the beach. He shared:

> I met a guy, a really good Thai guy, who said to make a rule for your life, like something that you do every day. He said to do something every day for yourself. So, I have my rule: I pretend that I don't have much money and that every day I have a budget of 100 baht to buy what I need for the day. But first, I need to do something to get the 100 baht, and if I don't, I cannot spend the 100 baht. And every day it is the same thing. These are the rules for me. Practice, that's what I do.

He continued, and explained precisely how he weaves this into his days, even when he travels between the islands:

> I think that the study life is harder than school. If you are smart, you cannot catch fish! Haha! Really, you can't catch fish to cook. If you can fish, you will have a lot of food and you can sell it. That's how you can get money. This is life. I just want to show you that every day, every moment, you can make money, and figuring out how to make money is easy. That is how I travel. Normally, when you are traveling you just sit on the bus and sleep. But I practice when I go traveling. I entertain people on the bus and the ferry, and also when they make stops. I might bring a flow art toy or a laptop so I can practice DJing, or I'll do magic tricks for people. Then, I might sleep a little and wake up in Bangkok, and I'll have my 100 baht for the day. Studying in the university only gives you one skill, but we can have other ideas and learn other skills with our hands. I have a lot of skills. You have to have skills to get money.

Having taken these journeys between islands and the mainland many times, I was amazed at how Som turned monotony into utility. I had never been on the bus-to-boat journey with Som, but I imagined him striking up conversations with tourists on the wide array of topics he could converse about and then moving in to show them a card trick. I thought about him at the rest stops on the side of lonely highways, outside the front entrance of the cafeterias where people gathered after getting their lunches, smiling at onlookers as he practiced his breakdance moves and *poi*. For Som, this was not necessarily busking with a full intention of making money, although it was clear that some of his quotidian practice did bring in tourist tips; this was not work, but practice, as he states above. Som's everyday practice was not necessarily driven by a search for money but a quest for the continued sense of security and comfort that came from knowing he could monetize talents and shape-shift the entertainer as needed. Som's immersion in the nightlife was something he saw as key to his ability to survive and thrive. The people he met and the skills he absorbed gave Som an edge. He was not just a fire dancer but an entertainer pursuing a study life.

Through my time around Som, I came to see how the elaborate set of toys followed him as insulators that could be utilized against the destructive forces that took down places like Mama's restaurant. As an entertainer, Som was flexible and could easily bend and twist into a new industry—massage, sewing, music-making, DJing—providing assurance that he could adapt comfortably to changing market trends. This was not work and not something he was forced to do as those in the factories but rather a self-directed practice of building a repertoire of tools. Indeed, they were tools that interested Som and that he liked—his talents—but they could also be deployed to generate income. Practice thus was a perspective that Som carried with him, itself providing a sense of ease in that he could adapt to spaces of tourism through the flexibility required to fit comfortably into changing economies and spaces. Som, the entertainer, was a connector in the tourism assemblage, a figure able to pull from surroundings to generate talents, new lives, and livelihoods. Som's pursuits were caught in between the anxieties of tourist economies—their lulls and uncertainties—and desires for the pleasure talents bring.

Becoming a *Manut*

Som's everyday practicing also spun him into new pursuits away from the tourist beaches, out of the quotidian ordinariness of Koh Samui, and into what Som believed were new realms of the extraordinary. He described how his ultimate dreams would take him out of the tourism industry as a laborer and transform him into a traveler. He elaborated:

> I have a lot of ideas, you know? I have two dreams: first is opening my own school; and second is traveling around the world to teach people what I know. I will show them all the things I have learned. We have another life, you know? It's my dream to travel around the world and to teach people what I do. I will go to another country, and they will give me a place to stay, and I will teach them. I will make all the people say, "Wow, this guy is cool. He can teach many things." In the future, I will make my school and maybe I can sell the toys I make. I will make a Facebook page called "Som Traveling around the World." If I have 1 million people and I sell each a toy for 200 baht, it means I get 200 million baht. That's a lot of money.

Som's dreams are intimately intertwined with skill diversification, practicality, and the knowledge needed to monetize talents. Som viewed himself as a traveler in-becoming, and it was clear from the way he interacted with tourists to learn new things and spent days outside the guesthouse practicing that he was somewhat already undergoing this transformation—moving from a dancer to someone with multiple talents who travels as he entertains, precisely because of his ability to draw in and connect his skills together. I think about this not only in terms of what Som was able to develop with card tricks, juggling balls, and flow art toys but also in the sense of his emotional skills such as his ability to converse with almost anyone on a range of topics and to pick up and remember new languages.

Som saw this future as something much more than fulfilling a desire to travel and teach; it was a pursuit through which he would change from a normal human into a "special" one and encourage others to do the same:

> My dream is to be a musician. Like making live music and DJing. And I want to make music to build people up like, "Wake up people" and to make people think, you know? I would use all my life skills to show them. I would teach them to be a special human, not a normal human. In Thai we say khon and manut. In English maybe it would be human and special human. So, khon means people who don't know what to do in life and just try and try. They don't know that what they are trying for is bad, that it is the wrong way, you know? But manut is someone who already knows about what life is, how to live life and be happy. It means happy people.

Som's translation of *manut* is precise and references a sense of spiritual wisdom. A *manut* is the opposite of the ordinary person (*khon*) and is applied to those "who have engaged in enough introspective spiritual practice to encounter and embrace wisdom. In Buddhism, humans have a *telos*—a potential state of perfection and goal of living—becoming an enlightened being, a person who has become one with the Buddhist teachings [*thamma*] freed from the cycle of suffering. *Manut*, then, is a person walking the path to his or her ultimate nature, interested in gaining wisdom to get there" (Stonington 2020, 119). Som's pursuits are richly laden with Buddhist ideologies, and to be a *manut* amounts to great social respect in Thai society. Som saw himself as that special person, having been transformed through his participation in touristic labor on the beaches and his drive to continue learning through the study life. His talents would thrust him toward a life away from this beach, where he could comfortably extend himself further into new spaces in the world; he would have enough talent to get money to live and travel yet also be able to move past attachments to money and fears of not having enough through an abundance of talents and wisdom. Yet Som's path toward being a *manut* is also highly influenced by the economic anxieties that fire dancers face. He calls on neoliberal ideologies of independence, self-sufficiency, and the monetization of the self to make himself more than a fire dancer.

I sensed during our conversations on skills and money-making that Som was indirectly commenting on how those with formal education, like myself, faced precarity. Som's comments gave me pause as I was compared with those who had diverse skill sets and abilities to survive through one's own means, such as the ability to fish. Indeed, I cannot fish and would struggle to survive in a such context, while Som could thrive. In our very last interview in 2016 I asked Som what he wanted me to know that we had not yet discussed. He gave me the following piece of advice: "You have to make yourself like a rainbow, like have many colors, you know? Be patient, never stop, and everything will be good. That's it." I often felt that Som was concerned that I may not be fulfilled, and he wondered aloud about what I would do for money after my research. While I was privileged to have a scholarship to study in Thailand, it was not lost on Som that finding a job after completing a PhD would be difficult. Som offered this advice to me regularly: to diversify my skill set and have more "colors," which would allow for different ways to make money beyond the scholastic institutions I was used to. On my final day in Koh Samui, Som gifted me a piece of quartz he had found and explained that it would bring me luck on my next steps and hopefully manifest opportunities for me.

Som did, indeed, realize his dream of traveling around the world. Along with some senior *farang* and Thai fire dancers who were among the originals in Thailand, Som was invited to travel and work in China for a month. He has since had many opportunities to live out the fruits of his study life and be a traveler who teaches others. For Som, it is not only fire dance or touristic labor that made this possible but rather his passion for the pursuit of diverse talents and his ability to secure income no matter the circumstances. This was a resourcefulness built through touristic labor and the insight and wisdom of the entertainer—an example of how "the nightlife can be useful for the day life."

STRIVING ON KOH PHI PHI

I began the long walk around the back of the busy tourist lanes toward Nam's shop in the Gypsy Village.[1] I was thankful not to have to dodge tourists, carts, and the shouts of people selling diving trips. My pace was slower and calmer as I gazed out at the lush green around me, a stark contrast to the shops, bars, and backpacker dorms that clog up the alleyways behind the overly developed area of Loh Dalum Bay. This was my fourth time on Phi Phi, and I had come to appreciate the ways in which quietness hid in small spaces on the island. I passed by the local market where Thai and Burmese workers collected food for their shared meals. I continued on and started to see more Thai Muslim women pushing their pancake carts to feed those laboring in shops and restaurants around the Gypsy Village. I arrived at Nam's shop, a one-room space where he also lived. The outside was rustic-looking, and he purposefully hung wood logs around the exterior to look like the old hippie rasta style, as he called it. I stepped over a couple of chickens and Nam's kittens and was transported to a different world.

The shop was filled with leather, artisan jewelry pieces, log seats, a guitar, and North American Indigenous dreamcatchers that hung all over the walls. Job2Do, a Southern Thai rasta reggae band, played in the background. Nam was sitting in front of the small fan that barely cooled the temperature as he carefully sewed a leather bag. He was preparing for the upcoming high season when (hopefully) more tourists would wander by his shop and purchase his wares. One of Nam's friends was sitting on the floor, and I took a spot on the couch beside his guitar. They ate and smoked marijuana together and offered me some. Together, we relaxed and fell into the beats of Job2Do. My body settled in a way it struggled to do in the early days of fieldwork on Koh Phi Phi, which has an intense speed with the continual arrival and departure of tourists. Nam explained one day as I rushed off to a meet someone for an interview that I needed to "take time" and "move slowly," so each afternoon I would slow down and sit with Nam as he worked and watched the changing tourist economies on Koh Phi Phi.

Koh Phi Phi Don

Few tourists made it to isolated Phi Phi until after 1998 when the movie *The Beach* was filmed in a nearby marine park, and Koh Phi Phi Don developed considerably after the release of this movie. The most significant year on the island, however, is 2004, which marks the December 24 Indian Ocean tsunami. The tsunami devastated the small island, and inhabitants often speak about history as starkly divided into only two different times: before the tsunami and after. Not only did people lose loved ones, homes, and businesses, but the rebuilding of Phi Phi continues to have long-lasting effects through an intensification of tourism with new economic landscapes to navigate.

Land prices on Phi Phi have appreciated dramatically since 1998; after the tsunami powerful officials and wealthy Thai elite began to claim ownership over some of the best pieces of land. Inhabitants who owned small businesses were forced away from the beaches, up into the mountains, and it is rumored that there were collusions between the Thai government and corporations to build large-scale developments along the best areas of beach (Cohen 2008). In turn, the damage to the ecosystem has been profound. The Department of National Parks often has to close the nearby island where *The Beach* was filmed to allow the ecosystems to recover from the 5,000 tourists who arrive daily. Nostalgia permeates conversations of the times before the tsunami, while a quietly accepted despair hangs over conversations about the present and future of Phi Phi. These temporal and affective divides are spatially mapped onto the physical geography of the island. Phi Phi has two large bays: Loh Dalum, which faces north, hosts large nightly beach parties, and is the area that has been most developed after the tsunami, lined with bars, backpacker dorms, hotels and numerous parties each evening; and Ton Sai, on the opposite side, a quieter area where the boats arrive and depart and which is home to the Gypsy Village. The different sides of Phi Phi are discussed at length by inhabitants. Most Thais who were there before the tsunami despise Loh Dalum Bay, often just referring to it as "the other side," while Ton Sai evokes an affective longing for the past.

Phi Phi's changes have happened through what Rob Nixon refers to as slow violence, that is, "a violence that occurs gradually and out of sight, a violence of

FIGURE 6.1.   Bucket Bar in alleyway behind Loh Dalum Bay, Koh Phi Phi.

delayed destruction that is dispersed across time and space, an attritional violence that is typically not viewed as violence at all" (Nixon 2011, 2). While the tsunami came in a quick spectacular burst, the aftermath of destruction has been slower and more diffuse. The mass number of tourists leaving garbage everywhere, the overflowing sewers, the never-ending new construction projects, the dying coral, and the endless comings and goings of boats leave the island on the brink of collapse. This environmental suffering is paralleled by the emergence of what Elizabeth Povinelli (2011) terms an economy of abandonment, in this case fueled by the capital of elite Thais and transnational corporations that have infiltrated the island, which leaves long-settled inhabitants unable to compete. Contemporary neoliberal biopolitics do not manifest through eventful spectacles that demand political urgency, but, like slow violence, through uneventful "ordinary suffering" (Povinelli 2011, 13–14); subjects marked as not valuable are slowly and quietly forgotten. In the midst of abandonment, people create various "social projects" to "capacitate an alternative set of human and posthuman worlds," yet they are met with forces that exhaust their efforts and that thrust their lives into a temporal zone of endurance (Povinelli 2011, 7). While Phi Phi's development has brought many more tourists, it has been increasingly difficult for the long-settled laborers and small business owners to survive in the intensified market. They must find new livelihoods in the midst of a slow violence that extracts capital and abandons those who have lived on the island for years.

The changes on Phi Phi have affected fire dancers profoundly, and they must find new ways to endure the economic and social changes ushered in by the tsunami's aftermath. Fire dancers' bodies have become sites onto which the anxieties surrounding Phi Phi's demise are projected. Unlike other areas in Thailand where dancers are constructed as sexual deviants, fire dancers on Phi Phi are associated with viral decay. The number of dancers on the small island has grown enormously in the past ten years to support the increased development of bars along Loh Dalum Bay. The fire shows that take place all along the beach mark the start of wild, loud, and intoxicated nightly beach parties that, for inhabitants, represent the demise of a once serene Phi Phi. The discussion with the Department of National Parks officer for Phi Phi that opens chapter 1 is but one example of how fire artists are blamed for the dirtiness of tourist beaches. A longtime French inhabitant told me of a member of the royal family who visited Koh Phi Phi and said that the island looked dirty; officials were directed to ban fire dancing in an effort to clean up the image. Moreover, Thai fire dancers' economic security has diminished significantly during the tourism expansion on Phi Phi. While the number of fire shows has grown, almost all of the dancers filling these roles are undocumented laborers from Myanmar. Thai fire dancers on Phi Phi have been quietly pushed out of the industry while younger Burmese dancers, who receive little pay and work under the control of powerful bosses, are offered most of the jobs. It is precisely these forms of unspectacular violence that Nam, a longtime Southern Thai fire dancer, negotiated on Phi Phi as he struggled to remain economically and socially valuable.

FIGURE 6.2. Fire dancers along Loh Dalum Bay, Koh Phi Phi.

Nam—A "Spicy South Thai Guy"

Nam was born and raised in a rural area in the southern province of Krabi and was in his twenties when we first met. He grew up poor in terms of economic capital but expressed that his life was rich in other ways, particularly in how his family caught fish, farmed, and lived off the land, practices he felt were rare in the current moment. Nam's father was a Muslim *Chao Le*, an identity Nam claimed for himself through the term "Sea Gypsy," and his mother a Buddhist from the southern mainland. He entered the tourism industry when he was quite young and worked numerous jobs—as a boat driver, waiter, bartender, and shop owner—but most of his life had been committed to fire dancing, which he had done for well over ten years on Phi Phi. Nam danced all over the island but had settled into quiet Ton Sai—on the opposite side of the island from newly developed Loh Dalum Bay—where he performed what is advertised as the last original fire show on Phi Phi. Nam's team were among the last Thai fire dancers on the island and danced at the only show on Ton Sai Bay. Some team members were in their thirties, which is considered quite old in the fire dance scene, and they were astutely aware that they would soon no longer be able to complete with the influx of younger dancers who charge less for their shows.

Looking out over Ton Sai Bay as he wove cotton around his long fire staff to prepare for the evening show, Nam stated, "It used to be hippie here. Everyone had big hair, dreadlocks and like rasta. All this side [Ton Sai]. The other side [Loh

Dalum] now it is crazy. Parties started on that side about three or five years ago. Many people from Myanmar came. Now it is the new style and if it is a new style, it is because they not from here. They come to work on Phi Phi because they want European girlfriends. But before, people came to work on Phi Phi because they wanted to help their family." Nam often used this language of "hippie" and "rasta" to describe the predevelopment times. Like other dancers, he transferred his anxieties about shifting economies and precarity onto the bodies of the dancers from Myanmar and "the other side." Moreover, his longing for a past prior to the extensive development of tourism is also projected on the landscape of Phi Phi and dancers. These temporal and spatial distinctions are woven through notions of ethnicity, gender, and sexuality. By delineating dancers—Thai and Burmese—Nam establishes differing moralized motivations of each group and positions himself in a particular way. Nam considered himself to be the last rasta on Phi Phi, an identity that referenced Thai rasta reggae music, and specifically the ethos of Job Bunjob, the lead singer of Job2Do. With his long dreadlocks, dark skin, and Southern Thai dialect, Job Bunjob wrote songs about the issues of Southern Thai people and produced political messages about environmental sustainability (Sawangchot 2013). Nam very much saw himself in this image— as a Southern rasta concerned about the destruction of Phi Phi. Most rasta fire dancers, Nam lamented, had left the island in recent years because of the emerging new style, a slow erasure that he felt paralleled other issues in the region he called home.

For Nam, the issues on Phi Phi were connected with larger erasures that happened through Thai nation-building projects. Thai identity (*ekka lak Thai*) emerged through a spatialized political process in the nineteenth century that created a "scheme of ethno-space" in which the elite in the Central region were positioned as *siwilai* (civilized) in opposition to those at the peripheries (Winichakul 2000, 55). This project of nation building attempted to cast Siam (as it was formally known) as *siwilai* to colonial powers, although it relied on forms of indirect colonization that resulted in a national identity privileging the languages, cultures, religion, and histories of the Central region, glossing vast linguistic, ethnic, cultural, and religious diversity (Herzfeld 2002; Loos 2006; Reynolds 2002; Winichakul 1994). A spatial politics of power persists in the contemporary moment that maintains beliefs that the Central is superior and modern compared with the peripheries, spatialized demarcations that affected Nam's life. About being a Sea Gypsy, he explained, "We are *chon klum noi*.[2] It means we are not big. Just only maybe 500 people that stay together. But the king in Thailand made everyone not be this." He continued, "They look at us like we have no money, like we are jungle boys. You have to have short hair and look like Chinese with white skin [to be respected]. Hahaha!" These forms of Thainess (*kwam pen thai*) were not readily performed by Nam's body, and he objected to these constructions by refusing Thainess; Nam embraced his "black" (*si dam*) skin, wore his hair "big," and proudly proclaimed himself as a Sea Gypsy, a jungle boy, and a rasta—descriptors that coalesced under the larger rubric of what he referred to as being a "South Thai guy."

Nam believed that South Thai guys possessed particular qualities and capacities that set them apart from others in Thailand, especially the new elite bar owners, businesspeople, and laborers who came from the central region to the southern region to extract capital through tourism industries. In comparing himself, he explained that "South Thai guys are *more* spicy." I asked for clarification, to which he laughed and replied, "Spicy, like we do so many things. We always go to many places. Spicy. Ya, spicy. Like a bad boy. Crazy. Ya, South Thai guy—That is why we can do many things." When I first met Nam, he joked that he and his friends were "spicy hot" guys, and I understood this as a playful moment with a tourist that engaged the eroticization of male fire dancers. It wasn't until many months later, however, as Nam got to know me as a researcher, that the layered meanings of Southern Thai spiciness were revealed. Nam took the deviancy that is associated with fire dancers, as well as constructions of Southern Thai men as "violent, clannish and aggressive" (Polioudakis 1991), and forged them into a resilient capacity to "do many things" in the midst of slow violence. Spiciness was not only a clever play on words but a resourcefulness that provided the affective thrust for Nam to contest abandonment and slow violence in creative and subtle ways.

Spicy Capacities

While Nam made little money from fire dancing at the only bar left on Ton Sai, he continued on in a very specific style with his fire staff as a way to contest this abandonment, enliven his spiciness, and manage his relationship with the changing industry. Fire dance shows in Thailand are typically improvised to DJ'd music with groups of dancers on the stage at once. However, Nam's show was thoroughly choreographed, and he and his five-man team went up one by one to perform a set routine. These individual performances were followed by tightly choreographed multiperson routines. The show was incredibly long, and I often noticed the dancers' physical exhaustion as they would begin dropping the equipment they danced with. While Nam emerged strong and in control of the fire staff in the early sets, two hours later, his body struggled to manipulate the equipment. Tourists sensed this exhaustion and often left before the tip bucket made its final round, which affected how much the dancers earned.

I was perplexed about why Nam and his team adopted this structure, since it was clear this style of performance meant they earned *less* and potentially pushed customers toward the other shows on Loh Dalum Bay. I came to learn, however, that this type of show was a platform where the forces of slow violence were mediated; it was a way in which Nam delineated his team's capacities from those dancing on Loh Dalum. He explained, "Here [Ton Sai] we each have our own style. There [Loh Dalum] everyone is the same. You know stick [fire staff]? I know about twenty-five moves. Over there, they only need to know about five and just do the same thing." This structure of performance was not about attempting to capitalize on tourism but was an attempt to showcase something he felt was unattainable by the new-style dancers. Nam explained that he went on stage by himself with his fire staff, spinning wildly and demonstrating great control and knowledge to showcase that he had his "own style" and could "do many things"—his spiciness.

Each evening, Nam performed to carry on the legacies of the South Thai guys who had been abandoned by the new-style economies, as he kept spicy affects alive through this type of fire dance, even though there were few tourists who even ventured to the bar. Through his dancing, he formed relational connections with South Thai guys, although in so doing he also projected the issues of abandonment onto the bodies of Burmese dancers rather than the wealthy bar owners who drive the economy of abandonment forward. The spiciness that comes to life through his fire staff mediates these power relations, while it also produces aspects of Nam's exhaustion—economic and physical. Nam danced with his staff each evening to embody and produce capacities to carry on in the face of the violence of erasure. Nam realized the futility in attempting to make money through these performances. So, he had other interventions through which he sought to survive economically while also practicing and generating spiciness.

> In Thailand they just want the people who are good at studying [go to school] and we are considered like jungle boys, us Sea Gypsies, you know? They [the state] don't care. We take care of the tourists. And they should care because we help make people who come to Thailand happy and spend money. But they do not see this. We do something for Thailand, but Thailand does not do something for us. Phi Phi is beautiful because of the coconut trees. When we no longer have coconut trees, Phi Phi will not be beautiful. If you have the land but no coconut trees, it's just the land. Same as if you do not have fire shows, no sea, no coral. Now we can see these things, but in fifteen or twenty years you won't see them. That is why I do something else. I have to help Thailand but also help myself too. That's why I make the shop, so I don't just only help Thailand.

Nam compared the destruction of ecologies to his own looming disappearance as a Southern Thai fire dancer. Nam, however, refused an easy abandonment and decided to proceed by turning his home into a shop.

Nam built his home, a small one-room wooden enclosure with a metal door, on a quiet path in the Gypsy Village far from the new development along Loh Dalum Bay. His home not only was a place to relax and have an interlude from the intense tourism on the island but was a space in which he drew on his abilities to do many things—creating jewelry and accessories to sell to tourists. Nam's home had become a conglomeration of his creations as well as found objects that he has collected over the years. It was filled with leather bags and wallets, with bracelets and necklaces hanging off the walls, various log seats on the floor, drawings and artwork, and a large collection of North American Indigenous-style artifacts that included an extensive collection of dreamcatchers that he made. It seemed as if something new would appear each time I went. Upon entering, I had to move carefully around guitars, jewelry, and art that hung on the walls, in the windows, and from the ceiling. Nam would spend his days in his home making inventory that crowded his living space and that adorned his home with a handcrafted and natural aesthetic he associated with rasta culture from earlier times on Phi Phi. His home-turned-shop was a direct contestation to the competitive fire dance industry he was being pushed out of, and Nam's life and work were enmeshed in the space as he tried to survive the economic shifts. The shop did not, however, possess great earning potential, as it struggled to compete with the multitude of other shops that had infiltrated Phi Phi, but it did provide a viable avenue for when Nam would officially be abandoned by the fire dance industry. The importance of the shop, however, went beyond economic survival; for Nam, the shop and its contents were avenues for contesting and reimaging histories and futures in the region.

Since Michel deCerteau's formative work on tactics of resistance in everyday life (1984), the quotidian and the mundane have increasingly been examined as important sites of political contestation for minoritized subjects (Ahmad 2016; Alexandrakis 2016; Das 2007; Howe 2016; Gammeltoft 2016; Mahmood 2005; Manalansan IV 2005, 2014). Given the dangers of social critique in Thailand, discussions of political life often take place through coded language, sounds, and material culture (Tausig and Haberkorn 2012; Tausig 2019). On a small island that is controlled by powerful elite families, Nam found creative avenues for subversive social projects that fueled and, in turn, were fueled by his spiciness. Nam's home was intensely crowded with art and objects and was an affective archive of a life forged in the midst of, and in response to, erasure. Martin Manalansan IV, through his look at the "messy" homes of queer immigrants of color in New York, argues that their collections of material items are archival practices for creating "spaces of fervently mobile fictions, tactics, and strategies" that enliven people's memories and their survival under oppressive social forces (2014, 157). The objects that clutter Nam's living space are generative platforms for ephemeral tactical maneuvers. Through objects and affects, Nam archives and animates his endurance as a spicy South Thai guy who resists the slow forces of abandonment.

I visited Nam's shop almost every day as a quiet time to relax from the bustle of tourists that filled the laneways on the island. Each time I visited, the laid-back reggae rhythms of Job2Do reverberated off the walls as Nam sat on one of the wooden logs and worked on his pieces. It was during his crafting that Nam would speak to me about all his skills that he had learned throughout his life, often pointing to the creations around his home. The pieces were evidence of Nam's continued resourcefulness, adaptability, and capacity to do many things. As he crafted, he would reflect on his childhood when he learned to farm and fish, skills that he characterized as being "much more difficult than fire dance" and that set him apart from the new-style dancers who he felt were closing him out of the industry. The skills he used in his shop to create objects and art also differentiated him from others on Phi Phi who, he believed, did not hold the knowledge he had. About Southern Thai men, he explained, "We learn by working. Not all people learn in school, you know? When I worked driving a long tail boat, I learned about fish, water, and mountains. And then I worked in the restaurant, and I learned about food. And then I worked in the bar, and I learned about everything. And after a long time, I put it all together and I can do many things." Nam was ambivalent about formal education, much like Som in chapter 5, and we often joked about how little I knew because I had spent far too much time in university. "I learn by looking. By myself," Nam would say, pointing to all of the objects he had figured out how to make and sell to tourists. As we had these conversations, we would sometimes glance across the path from his doorway at the large tourist resort that had been recently built, and Nam would comment on how one needs a "certificate" (degree) to work there, which he did not have. His spicy skills, in contrast, were developed through laboring and self-determination, and he used this differentiation to position himself in distinction from those in the elite and middle classes who occupied higher positions in the national imaginary and who were the leaders of the new-style economy on Phi Phi.

His shop was an archive of skills developed outside of, and in opposition to, formal educational institutions. Nam believed that institutional knowledge focused too much on technological development and commerce, which had left the ecologies in the region on the brink of collapse. He explained, "University teaches everyone the same. Everyone studies technology. We don't need this. They don't know what to do about working in the jungle, about the sea. They only know the city." Nam's comments responded to the fast-paced development on the island, which greatly transformed the economies and ecologies. Nam frequently talked about how Phi Phi's demise was because those in positions of power may have had certificates but did not possess the rural jungle and sea skills that he held. It was clear that he felt Phi Phi could benefit from the spiciness of South Thai guys rather than the credentials and capital of elites. His shop became a space closed off from the knowledge certificates generate and was cluttered with things he had learned to make through working his various jobs. While such spicy resourcefulness might not be valued by the elite Thais who shape Phi Phi's future, Nam reimagined this hierarchy of value in his shop. His home was an archive of his resiliency as well as a space that valued his knowledge, rather than that held by those with extractive desires that fueled the tourist industry that was quietly destroying his island home.

Chut Mung Mai

The objects in Nam's home did not only showcase and value spicy skills but also contained stories of how Nam gained this spiciness through affiliations and kinships that contest official histories of Thainess and the "genealogical grids" that had been ascribed to him (Povinelli 2002). What I first noticed upon entering Nam's shop is that it was filled with Indigenous dreamcatchers and other art pieces in, very broadly, a North American Indigenous style. In turn, photographs of North American Indigenous people hung all over the walls. Upon my asking where he got the photographs, Nam pointed to one and stated jokingly through laughter, "My uncle." As Nam was making a dreamcatcher one day, I asked why he liked this style, and he explained,

> South Thai guys like *Indian Daeng* [Red Indian] style. South Thai guys are very strong like a Red Indian, you understand? They have strong hearts, and they want to do something. Like spicy! Haha! Red Indian people, they are spicy. South Thai guy and *Indian Daeng* people have *chut mung mai*; this means like when you want to do something and you know what is going to happen in the future and you want to do it, so you can get to the dream. Like when you want to do something, and you don't stop. You want to make something better or when you have a competition, and you want to win and you just try everything to win.

Chut mung mai translates as the hope to get to a certain point and of having a goal that one continues to strive for. It was deeply connected to spiciness for Nam; it expressed not only a type of resourcefulness but the endurance to persist, learn, and adapt one's skills to changing situations with a hopeful future as a goal. It was clear that Nam had a felt affiliation with *Indian Daeng* and his work in this aesthetic complemented his Southern Thai spiciness with a will to continue being valuable and visible. These pieces and the embodied acts of creating them, however, held a much deeper meaning to Nam, as they provided a platform for what he called a "secret culture" to persist despite much longer forms of abandonment and erasure.

Unlike the other crafts Nam made, he insisted that knowledge of North American Indigenous dreamcatchers was not something he learned through working but that it "comes from my blood because I never learned it; I just can do it." He described how these *da kai chap fan* (net for catching dreams) were constructed similarly to the nets they made for fishing in his home village, although this was not an aesthetic coincidence. As we sat one day, Nam pulled out a container with beads that he used to decorate some of the dreamcatchers. He dumped the beads in his hand and said, "2,500 years old." He proceeded to tell me a story of a boat that had come to Southern Thailand 2,500 years ago that was filled with treasures. Nam explained that the boat sank very close to shore. The people on the boat survived, and the treasures and artifacts drifted to the mainland. He stated, "Red Indian and Apache people came with the boat. We found stones that look like they come from Red Indian people." Nam and his friends would find these artifacts from time to time along the beaches when they were young. The beads he used on his dreamcatchers, he insisted, had come from that boat and were evidence of untold relations that were part of Nam's history. Nam described the boat as a micro-cosmopolitan formation that had people on it from all over the world who had all settled in the South of Thailand. These diverse ethnocultural groups had mixed over many years: "Here we have many different cultures and mix mix mix for one thousand years. I am like five mixtures together."

Nam was quick to caution me about the larger forces that seek to silence this knowledge and history. He explained,

> What I tell you is secret culture. In Thailand we have a good king and my king just wants to forget about who came from there, there, there [different places]. My king told the teachers not to teach us about our own separate cultures because maybe we will have bad memories and then we will fight. I never learned this in the school. I think in Southern Thailand we have a sad culture. The king didn't want to make me and my friends in school sad and want to fight Thailand. The teachers in Thailand cannot tell you what I am saying, because they only learn about the culture from North of Thailand. But we are from Southern

Thailand. When I was young, I never thought about why my teacher didn't tell me about my culture. But when I got older, I see everything. And then I wanted to know about my culture too, but now I don't want to know. Because if I know, maybe it will make me get sad and get angry with Thailand. And I don't want to get angry. I don't want to know.

Thailand, and particularly the South, is not accurately represented by the homogenized Central "Thai" that is narrativized in schools, in books, and in the media, a history that erases the complexity of Nam's experiences and culture as a South Thai guy, specifically. This conversation was carefully negotiated by Nam and me because of how it troubles official accounts. I wondered if Nam was performing a heritage to make his Indigenous crafts seem more authentic, as he understood authenticity as a desire of tourists. While I have not been able to find any documentation of the story of the boat, I do not believe the truth of this story is what is important; the story was true for Nam and me in our encounters, and for the connectivities and histories it enlivened. It was, in turn, a way for Nam to engage in modes of resistance that permeate Thai social life and involve changing how one feels about a particular issue, as an act of letting go (*ploy wang*) and "emotionally coming to terms with an event" (*tham jai*) rather than engaging in direct confrontation (Cassaniti 2015b, 284).

Instead of tracing and recouping Nam's history through biological grids, we must give space for considering kinship and connections among people dispersed across transnational spaces as *felt* materialities that are no less real than those based on genetic material. David L. Eng argues that vast migrations and new forms of social belonging "have demanded consideration of how contemporary evolutions in the meanings and values of social organization and community are, in Raymond William's terms, 'actively lived and felt' as structures of feeling" (2010, 2). By employing the lens of queer diaspora, Eng considers heritage and kinship as affective—that is, "not in conventional terms of ethnic dispersion, filiation, and biological traceability, but rather in terms of queerness, affiliation, and social contingency" (Eng 2010, 13). This framework helps to unpack the relations Nam claims. While Nam stated that his affiliation with North American Indigenous people was "in his blood," this is primarily a felt connection he claimed through what he understood as a shared spiciness and *chut mung mai*. For Nam, "blood" was an affective material that provided an endurance to persist and not the genetic substance of proof. Nam's playful joking about the photograph in his home of an Indigenous man that was his uncle does not undermine the connection. Rather, Nam joked about this because he knows such an affiliation would not be legible within normative frames.

These artifacts and art supported Nam's refusal of official notions of Thai heritage, as well as his coming to terms with it. He did not attempt to mend a fragmented history; he reinvented one that spilled outside of neat categorizations and legible clean lines of descent. In so doing, Nam invites us to understand messy connections that are in excess of genetic material and that unite people across spaces and times in ways that defy organizational knowledge and, instead, operate as "intangible areas of social existence and belonging" (Eng 2010, 15). Nam's history of the boat urges an opening of the parameters of kinship to allow for genealogical arrangements that "mess up" tidy histories, connections, and lives through their refusal to be neatly organized (Manalansan IV 2014). The dreamcatchers are potent sites of memory that support an enduring kinship based in spiciness and *chut mung mai*. The stories these objects generate through the small, beaded decorations that are woven into their webs hide a secret culture and affiliations that continue to persist in the face of abandonment, and that, for Nam, contributed to the spiciness that has supported his endurance as a South Thai guy on Koh Phi Phi.

Rather than an intervention that is framed within a temporality of stasis, unable to wrest itself from forces of exhaustion, Nam's home and dancing were productive sites of creative material maneuvers through which he refused abandonment. Nam used his crafts and artifacts to position himself differently in the new-style economies on Phi Phi; his rural skills and long histories of spiciness provided the resilience to persist, but through crafting, dancing in his own style, and decorating his home, he produced value for his own sets of knowledge. Nam's quiet and affective contestations are not sites of inevitable despair caused by ever-increasing neoliberal capitalism in the tourism industry but generative practices in which his endurance and striving reject economies of abandonment and create new possibilities and futures to thrive. Nam's crafting supported his ability to remain viable by providing income in a changing fire dance market, but his objects and art also recomposed histories and power relations. Nam asserts himself as more valuable and knowledgeable than those who come from beyond the southern regions and who are seductively drawn to Phi Phi by desires to extract capital and resources from a region that people have long inhabited.

While not minimizing the violence of tourism industries, it is important to consider the creative ways that people survive hopefully in the midst of economic and social abandonment. Nam drew on a spiciness that has been long embodied by South Thai guys, and he adapted to the changing circumstances of tourist Phi Phi. His felt connections with *Indian Daeng* secured Nam in affective solidarities across spaces and times with others who he believed became resourceful and persisted in the face of violence and erasure. The material clutter of Nam's home was imbued with and productive of these stories and connectivities that have endured violent pasts and that inflect futures on Phi Phi with a "cautionary hopefulness" that despite ecological, economic, and social abandonment, life will continue to strive forward (Manalansan IV 2005, 157).

7

FIRE DANCE FEMININITIES

As I was practicing and learning with Neo, who danced with Nam on Koh Phi Phi, he started to show me the way he felt my body should move with *poi*. He picked up my toys and quickly embodied a graceful flow. As his face softened, he presented a slight smile and moved with my *poi* with incredible grace, interspersing tricks with the slow movement of limbs to accentuate his body. He explained that this was the "girl" style of fire dance, which I embody even though the great majority of my teachers were men. I asked, "Why are there no female Thai fire dancers?" This was the very first question that started my engagement with fire art in Thailand in 2010, and I posed this question to every dancer who would speak to me. As it turns out, I received a very simple answer in the form of a question from Neo in reply: "Everyone learns from friends. Who would teach them?"

While I was well connected with the vast majority of fire dancers around Thailand, I only ever heard of three Thai women who still danced, Dao, Kat, and Khao, and only a handful of *farang*. I saw no others, particularly in the new generation. Given that this form of fire art almost everywhere else in the world involves women and that women were involved in the early days of flow art, I was perplexed at how this had become a male art form in Thailand. This chapter explores the gendering of the genre through speaking with female fire dancers, both Thai and *farang*. It examines how certain figures, imaginaries, and histories dwell and lurk at the edges of the fire dance scene and illicit uncomfortable affects. Given that most of the book has been heavily centered in male voices and perspectives, here I have featured separate conversations with different women in the scene to show the diverse ways in which women navigate this male world and the affects within it. The voices of women reveal how they negotiate fire dance labor vis-à-vis social mores concerning femininity in Thailand. I also include my own experience moving and being in fire communities as a female researcher to highlight how the possibilities for female participation are negotiated in this scene vis-à-vis more widely circulating images and narratives about Thai and *farang* women.

As has been discussed in previous chapters, gender in Thailand is a fluid conception, captured succinctly through Penny Van Esterik's notion of a gendered surface that one shifts and changes through behavior, appearance, comportment, speech, style, and a range of other practices (2000). Understanding and *doing* gender in this way, however, require knowledge of *kalatesa*—temporal and spatial context—and this is crucial for women, especially. Van Esterik explains:

> *Kalatesa* is very much concerned with surfaces, with appearances, but in Thai society these surfaces matter. Knowledge of *kalatesa* is expressed through dress, language, and manner. . . . Topics of conversation must also suit the time and place, such as appropriate conversation topics for meals, for mixed company. If you hear a personal conversation, you should withdraw. You were in the wrong space and time. Surely this is equally true in polite Canadian settings. "Yes," said my Thai friend, "But in Thailand the lapses (*phit kalatesa*) matter more." Someone who violates *kalatesa* loses face and respect (*barami*). (2000, 39)

Kalatesa represents a coming together of time and space that determines what is possible in a particular moment; the creation of a gendered surface might involve slight changes to physical appearance, language, tone of voice, and a multitude of embodied gestures and prescriptions that can vary based on context. While this is not directly discussed by Thais, it is very much known. Over the years, Thais have helped me shape my body and behavior without ever explaining why certain modes of dress, voice, gesture, and language were better in some contexts than others; they were teaching me *kalatesa*. While *kalatesa* and gendered surfaces showcase great fluidity in personal presentation and the relationality of the self, wider static constructions of gender and sexuality—national and transnational—influence surfaces and must be carefully negotiated by Thai women.

We cannot begin to discuss Thai femininities without considering how the circulation of images of Thailand has impacted gendered and sexual constructions in the country. The Thai government has sought for decades to reverse its sexualized image through the careful control of the country's external presentation, even while sex tourism continues to be a very lucrative industry. The branding of

Thailand as a "sex scape" (Brennan 2004) has deeply affected the way that Thai femininities are discussed in the media, academia, and beyond: "The gendered and sexualized image of the Thai female prostitute dominates Western perceptions of gender analysis on Thailand," creating a "collapsing of Thai femininity with prostitution" (Jackson and Cook 1999, 13).

These problematic linkages create what Jin Haritaworn argues is a haunting of Thai femininities by the figure of the prostitute (2011). The ever-present figure also haunts the fire dance scene. Like the beach boy that male fire dancers contend with, particular figures lurk at the edges of Thai female fire dancers' surfaces but are not always stated outright. This is a complex haunting that evolves from not only the external sexualized imaginaries of Thailand but also national ideals surrounding female respectability. The stakes in the contextual sensitivity of doing gender for Thai women are high; women's bodies carry the "burden of representation" as symbols of national identity (Yuval-Davis 1997, 45).

Thai women have been implicated in national economic policies and the creation of governmentalized public images that seek to counter the sexualization of the country. The post-1997 financial crisis resulted in the "sufficiency policy" promoting moral principles of economic moderation so that everyone had "enough" (*pho phiang*), and affected how sexuality and gender were policed in public spaces. The bodies of nonbinary individuals, queer people, and women were scrutinized in new ways, while liberal discourses about sexual rights and democracy in the public sphere clouded the bodily restrictions that were taking place under the rubric of *pho phiang* (Fuhrmann 2009). These new nationalist policies and moral disciplinary campaigns "relied on anachronisms that were anchored in bodies and sartorial detail. Female bodies, especially, now figured as a baseline cultural good, a kind of heritage" (Fuhrmann 2009, 225). Indeed, this continues; the ideal Thai woman is expected to be modest, graceful, beautiful, and chaste. Given that fire dance was taking root in Thailand during the exact time that these notions of moderation were influencing economic and public policy, participating in fire art may not have been an acceptable form of public display even from the outset. Fire dance requires little clothing, lounging in tourist areas where people are typically drinking alcohol, and moving one's body in ways that might be considered immodest. This type of public control over women's bodies in performance is prevalent and has been reinvigorated under the ruling military regime. In 2017, *Luk Thung* (Thai country) singer Lamyai was scolded by General Prayuth, the junta leader, for her revealing clothing and "sexy" dance moves. Her manager offered a public apology and assured the media that this would change (Coconuts Bangkok, 2017).

Because of the importance of maintaining public appearance, spaces in which sexuality is openly expressed, such as the iconic sex districts in Bangkok, come to be associated with immorality, and thus those who work within them are often stigmatized, and this is particularly so for Thai women (Wilson 2004; Sinnott 2013). While there is a significant amount of domestic travel in Thailand and younger Thais do frequent some tourist entertainment areas, women are not usually present, and if they are, it is in a group. Female tourists are not subject to the same types of social rules, but it was a point of great concern for my Thai friends that I went out alone (*khon diao*), particularly to the tourist beach parties. As discussed in chapter 2, the tourist beach parties where fire dancing takes place are an ambivalent site for Thais because they are eroticized zones. Of course, sometimes there are Thais at beach parties, although it is rare at the tourist bars, but I have yet to see a group of Thai women alone at any beach party. The spatiotemporal context provides a substantial reason as to why there are not more Thai women who fire dance. While male dancers have to negotiate this stigma, these mediations are significantly more pronounced for Thai women. There were more Thai women in the first generation, although not many, and it was clear from discussions that male fire dancers welcomed female participation but that reinvigorating the scene to be more gender balanced was challenging.

Neo's reply to my question that opens this chapter provided a simple answer to my inquiry into why there were not more Thai women involved; social relations in Thailand are typically organized homosocially. If a man and a woman are hanging out together in public, it is usually because they are intimately involved or related. This is, of course, a generalization, but a woman alone in the company of men who is not one of their partners can draw negative attention. Thus, a Thai woman would likely not be able to learn from a Thai man whom she was not romantically involved with. Indeed, out of the three Thai female fire artists who are featured here, two—Dao and Khao—had learned directly from their male partners. Another dancer, Kat, learned in the park with Pi Neung, although her foray into the fire dance industry in the South was with her *farang* boyfriend. I was the only woman among those I met who was learning from men whom I was not in an intimate partnership with. And even with my *farang* privilege, my femininity could only be extended so far into this world. Below, I share the perspectives of four female fire dancers in Thailand—three Thai and one *farang*—to elucidate how they negotiate gendered surfaces and *kalatesa* (attention to time and place). I also share my own experience navigating this scene and learning *kalatesa*.

Kat

I met Kat through a *farang* female dancer in Bangkok, Celine, who is featured below. Kat was in a transition stage in 2016, having taken a break from the fire art scene in the Southern tourist hub of Phuket. She was known as one of the best dancers in Thailand. She was popular internationally, and was known by every dancer I spoke with in the first and second generations. I hung out with Kat each time I passed through Bangkok from 2016 and 2019, and we became friends. She is a fun-loving person, and we often went out for dinners, drank wine together, chatted, and went out to clubs and markets with her friends, many of whom were *farang*. She had recently broken up with her *farang* boyfriend when we first started spending time together, and she dreamed of having a family and a more settled life. When I visited again in 2019, Kat had not returned to fire dancing and instead had remained in Bangkok working jobs in the film industry and taking care of her mother.

Kat had learned with Pi Neung at the park in the early days, and even then, was the only girl. About why she started, she stated, "I was fascinated with fire dancing, and I think everyone who decided to spin fire has that same fondness that I felt when I first saw the moves." I asked how she felt about being the only female at the park, and she replied, laughing, "Oh, I don't mind. I like it. I always prefer to have more guy friends than girlfriends—less drama, you know? I am more like a boyish girl. It's more comfortable that way. They are not like girls, you know?" Kat understood herself as possessing a different type of femininity than the dominant Thai ideal, which was born from her struggles and experiences in fire communities. Kat explained that initially she had to fight her way into the fire scene, sometimes only being allowed to perform for ten minutes during a show of all men. It is a "protected" genre, she explained, and was viewed as "a man's thing to do," so Kat had to work hard to be accepted and gain access. The independent femininity she gained that allowed her access to the fire scene, however, caused her to clash with people in other social realms. She related that she could not play what she referred to as the "damsel in distress" that she felt her male work colleagues expected at her job in Bangkok, and thus, she was not accepted in the office environment. What Kat references here is the ideal of female respectability and femininity that she struggles to embody. Indeed, Kat was clear that she only dated *farang* men, and she related that Thai men never ask her out. She explained that she could not fit the Thai feminine ideal that a Thai man would want.

Kat was well aware of how external imaginaries of Thai female sexuality impacted the lives of Thai women. She remembered being aware of these problematic images since very young and characterized herself as somewhat protective about it. We were speaking one day about an expat magazine that had featured an article on "happy ending" massages, which refers to Thai massages for men that end with sexual play and orgasm. She commented on how such articles bothered her, as they perpetuated the continued association of Thailand with sex, a linkage that had deeply impacted her life. Kat made a lot of money as a fire dancer in Phuket, and from her other job as a reporter and event organizer, and this drew suspicion from those around her; Thai people, she felt, assumed she was a sex worker. She struggled with how fire dance was sexualized through these imaginaries:

> KAT: Usually people who come to Thailand are either running away from something or seeking something new. I think Thailand in general is already fascinating for people, and they think there are no rules in this country. I think that already is mind blowing for people and then they come to the South and see some sexy skinny brown guy fire spinning and are like, "Oh my god." Usually sex is the drive. Sex is behind everything.
>
> AUTHOR: Did you ever feel like that when you were dancing?
>
> KAT: A lot of people interpret it that way. Like, "Oh it's so sexy." I'm like—no. I guess it's because when females do it, it's sexy in that kind of form which I can relate to. But at the same time, I don't want it to be interpreted as sexy. That's why I don't like performing at the clubs. Because everyone is there for clubbing and fire art is just additional fun for them. That is not fulfilling for me. I sweat and bleed for this art.

The clubs Kat speaks of are the large bars that host beach parties on Phuket with heavy drinking and partying tourists. For Kat, being just "additional fun" for people was problematic. She wanted her art form to be watched and appreciated, but in a more attentive, and less sexualized, way. As we will hear from other women featured below, the association of dance with sexuality is highly ingrained in Thailand.

Kat developed strategies and surfaces to mitigate and deal with this sexualization, although they conflicted with other aspects of her personal beliefs and morals. Kat characterized herself as a hippie. She often talked about current political issues, capitalism, and corporate greed. For Kat, ideals such as sharing (*baeng pan*), living off the land, and being kind to others were rules to live by, and she often used her Facebook account as a tool for spreading such messages. Yet one of the ways in which Kat has found fulfillment as an artist has been through what she calls "going corporate," although this clashes with some of her own anti-capitalist desires. Kat found that performing outside of beach clubs, in hotels and wealthy elite establishments, mitigated the sexualized aspect of performances, but she was conflicted about how this might commercialize fire art and move it even further away from the principles of sharing that the park group had established. In fact, Kat was one of the pioneering fire artists to bring fire art into five-star venues in Thailand and explained,

> I think this is the part where artists and commercial art take a different stance. Because a lot of my artist friends who actually do really good art don't want to make it commercial because they don't want to lose their soul. But when you swallow the fact of that—the commercial factor—you don't have to see people getting drunk and wanting to get laid every single day. That is not fulfilling for me. I'm a hippie. I would rather walk barefoot and put flowers in my hair or something and grow my own food. I had to do a full two full years in the clubbing scene in the tourist part of Phuket, which is annoying, and which is what burned me out, I think.

Like those at the fire art center on Koh Samui from Pi Neung's lineage, Kat struggled with how the form had changed from a participatory practice to an economic enterprise. But her ability to sell expensive shows to hotels and private parties, outside of the beach parties, was something she came to appreciate, and this new context changed the way her femininity was understood. In her choice to book these types of exclusive events, she would often laugh and refer to herself as a "corporate bitch," which helped to hold the figure of the prostitute at bay.

Kat felt that this sexualized aspect equally applied to men but that they might not be as exhausted by it as she was. She was always very clear in explaining that both male and female fire dancers are not motivated to begin doing fire art because of the potential for sexual intimacies with *farang*, in the same way that the male fire dancers I spoke with insisted. But she stated, "They [men] would enjoy it more. I think for guys it's always cool to have so many girls. It's the opposite for girls." I questioned why she thought this was different, and she explained:

> I think because it's harder for guys to get laid. Also, it's part of natural behavior, you know? Men have to span their wings to get attention, you know, like attraction. They have to try to impress you. Because for girls we always have people approaching. So, I guess for the guys in the beach bar when you do something cool, a lot of girls will come to you. It's part of the game.

She reiterated that even though sexuality might be present, and perhaps more welcomed by men, it was not a reason why anyone would start to fire dance. Rather, she felt, it was a desire for a different sort of life outside the conventional nine-to-five schedule that was a key motivator. It is interesting to note, however, that Kat did see differences in how sexual attention might be enjoyed. While men spoke less directly about *not* wanting their bodies to be eroticized, they, like Kat, also attempted to move sexualized constructions that cast them as desiring of *farang* away from their bodies. In turn, men did not have to negotiate the same haunting of the prostitute and national ideals that seek to control public images of women, although they must negotiate the unacceptability of their labor and the beach space through the figure of the beach boy. For Kat, moving away from the beach party scene, a context that is laden with sexuality, and "going corporate" offered a level of respectability that she was more comfortable with. This came at the expense of her hippie ideals, but it allowed her to be fulfilled through her art.

Khao

I met Khao at Santichaiprakarn Park in Bangkok, which continued to be a hub for people to meet and play flow art, although very few still went there regularly. While not an original park dancer from Pi Neung's group, Khao was one of the people involved, alongside two *farang* expats, in managing a Facebook page and hosting meetups at Santichaiprakarn Park and at Benjasiri Park, which is far away from the backpacker district in the wealthy area of Sukhumvit Road. This group did not regularly meet while I was there, and it was more so by chance that one might find another flow artist at the park. I only ever met four of the dancers, but the group's social media accounts provided a platform for travelers to connect with others in the city. On the occasions I met Khao at the park, there was usually a tourist there who had contacted her through this group. We often practiced together and shared moves and techniques much like the early days when Pi Neung would play there. Khao's partner was a *farang* flow artist originally from the United States who had been living in Thailand for many years. She learned from him and from YouTube videos. Originally from the Northeast, Khao lived a privileged lifestyle in Bangkok and was a teacher at an international school. She regularly traveled to different countries and had extensive holidays. While not a performer, Khao was still considered to be quite good and was friends with Dao and Nah at the studio on Koh Samui.

Like Kat, Khao recognized herself as different from other Thai woman, and her sartorial practice also indicated this to me; Khao always wore a tight tank top that showed her midriff, which is uncommon, as it is not *riap roi* for Thai women, especially in public. Her embodiment of an atypical femininity was made clearer during an encounter with one of the original park dancers from the 1990s, Kai from Japan, who was there practicing one day with us. He was showing me some different moves and then went up to Khao to adjust her style.

He advised that she stand differently, with her legs straight and more posed for "*phu ying* style" (girl style). She replied that she likes "*phu chai* style" (guy style) because she has learned from men. Kai posed in *phu ying* style to show her and did some graceful movements with his chest, like waves up to the sky, insisting that her style should be changed. Khao just brushed it off, laughed, and continued doing her tricks in *phu chai* style.

We spoke more about this encounter later that evening when we went to the tourist area of Khao San Road for dinner. She explained that female style is smooth, beautiful, and slow and has more bodily movement, sometimes with only a few tricks. Indeed, I had heard this from Som at the center and Neo on Koh Phi Phi, who both indicated that the focus on complicated tricks was more for men. This reminded me, generally, of idealized female bodily practice and gesture, always so graceful, slow and deliberate, and of great importance in Thailand; my supervising professor in Thailand had worked extensively with me in this regard concerning language—her concern was not with how I pronounced specific Thai words but the grace with which I would say them and the slight gestures I did with my hands and lips. Khao said that she was mostly around men in the fire dance scene, and this influenced her style, gestures, and personality:

> KHAO: Ya that's why I look like a guy now, my personality haha! Like, the Japanese guy came to me and said, "Can you do this like the girl move?" No. I can't. I totally like the guy moves. I don't care. I only just like guy moves. I don't really care. I just want to spin like a guy. Because I don't want to pretend. Understand, I can be beautiful, but I don't want to do that. It is beautiful but I like to spin fast a little bit.
>
> AUTHOR: Was he telling you to pose in a certain way or something?
>
> KHAO: Ya, like in a Chinese or Japanese style, like ballet. They pose straight. But I'm not like this.
>
> AUTHOR: Right, you learned from men.
>
> KHAO: Ya, and I watched a lot of men on YouTube. I didn't watch girls on YouTube—it's more slow, smooth, and with maybe more body movement. It looks nice. But there are also many girls who do many tricks very well also. But most of those girls are in Europe and America.

Interestingly, what Khao describes as the female style is the aesthetic of slow flow that the center dancers in chapter 3 spoke of. For her, however, there was a gendered, national, and racialized dynamic to this aesthetic, and one that she does not want to always embody. This is different from how flow was rendered at the center, where it was an embodied politics of moral artistry. For Khao, it was an Asian female aesthetic—"Chinese" or "Japanese"—that she juxtaposed with *farang* women who also do many tricks, but in a way that was more akin to the guy style. Khao did not see herself, nor did she embody, the essentialized Asian female aesthetic that men asked of her. It was, however, precisely a certain type of *phu chai* (guy) aesthetic that had at first deterred her from trying flow art, an aesthetic of fastness and power that she associated specifically with men on the islands.

Khao explained that her *farang* boyfriend's style was much slower and calmer and that this is what initially drew her to the art form: "He is American, so it's very interesting for me because the Thai style of fire dancing is also different. A lot of guys do it, so not a lot of girls. So, I wasn't interested in that. They didn't inspire me. When I was in the islands, I saw the guys doing fast fire spinning and I thought this was not a girl thing." Seeing the style of her *farang* boyfriend, however, and then finding artists she liked on YouTube helped her to find the style that worked for her. There are clear disconnects and inconsistencies in the conversations, particularly concerning her preferred aesthetic; while Khao liked her *farang* female-influenced *phu chai* style in the presence of Japanese dancer Kai, and refused to change, it also seemed that particular forms of softness and slowness had initially attracted her to flow art and made her feel that there was space in the dance form for her to learn. For Khao, these differentiations in style were not only gendered but also linked with social class, and the islands were a space for a type of *phu chai* style that she did not like. She stated,

> I mean on the islands it is a different style. On the islands they don't really do the YouTube thing or sharing different movements. People in Bangkok, in the city, are different. They learn from people who are traveling around the world, and they also learn from YouTube so there are new movements all the time, new tricks all the time. So, people [in the city] can be experts more than those on the islands and learn faster, and learn different things and different styles. But, on the islands people just don't really care about those things. If they get to learn new things, they learn from people, like other people coming through, but only sometimes. In Bangkok there are different styles, different props [equipment]. You're not going to see many island people do something like that. And they [island dancers] like to spin very fast. But one thing in how they are different is that they are so full of power, so much energy, crazy energy. Yes, there are more men doing the fire thing because I think it looks dangerous and girls do not want to try. But if it is in this style [city style], girls might be interested to try because they don't see it as harmful, or very crazy or very fast. They might think, "Ok I can do it." And it's beautiful. It doesn't look like crazy spinning.

Khao expresses a cosmopolitanism that is possessed and embodied by city spinners like herself—a style that is born from interactions with foreigners and
transnational connections through the Internet that she felt were lacking on the
islands. It is also gendered in that the island style leaves no room for women in
Khao's opinion; it is a faster and more powerful *phu chai* style. These renderings
of difficulty, speed, and hardness of the island spinners, as juxtaposed to the
slower and more graceful styles of the city, reverberate with more widespread
regional gendered discourses that position Southern Thai men as rough, hard,
and aggressive (Kang 2014; Polioudakis 1991). The slowness of the *farang* city
style, and now the *farang phu chai* style, is what drew her into the art form. Unlike Kat, Khao did not characterize herself as a hippie but rather made very clear
distinctions of herself as a city person, an aspect that has influenced how she
learned her style of fire dance. The islands, she felt, were a space of men, while
the city spinning community was more welcoming of females and their style,
even if that *phu ying* style was influenced by more masculine tricks and *farang*
female artists. The men Khao learned from were not Thai but *farang*, and thus,
this ideal of a city *phu chai* style is also racialized and feminized.

Khao did not comment on the sexualized aspect of fire dance for women. She
did, however, indicate that the sexual associations around fire dancing were a
reason there were so many males, repeating an oft-heard discourse that fire dancers are very critical of:

> Khao: Can I tell you too about why there are so many guys? For guys,
> the first thing is that it looks cool for them. And they want a girl who
> will say, "Oh my god! Oh my god!" [motions about women watch-
> ing them]
> Author: I wonder why women like to watch.
> Khao: I don't know either! They go crazy and they like them! Many
> friends of mine sleep with different girls every night. I don't know,
> really. I think they just want to have a good time, and this is maybe
> something they have never seen in their home [country]. Because
> normal people don't go out and don't really see something like this.
> And then when they see something like this they are like, "Oh this
> made my day. This is amazing!" So, I don't know, but all my friends—
> the guys on islands—get a girl almost every day. What am I going
> to get if I'm a girl spinning fire? Hahaha! But all [girls] get so drunk.
> Hahaha! So drunk, they say like "He's so good. He's so sexy!" It is so
> funny. But all my friends got very hot girls. Ya, the Thai guys got very
> hot foreigner girlfriends.

What Khao is referring to is what Som describes as "the system of the bar" in chapter 1. Of course every Thai male dancer spoke back to these constructions and said that such discourses were a fabrication of their true intentions. For Khao, though, she felt otherwise, and I believe this also had to do with Khao's higher socioeconomic positioning in Bangkok. Her rendering of *farang* women as beautiful reverberates with wider Thai beliefs that position light skin and Caucasian women as desirable, but interestingly she also characterizes *farang* as excessive and out of control; they are "so drunk" and very explicit in their sexual attraction to Thai men, forms of public display and behavior that are very much un-Thai, particularly for women.

Because of her positioning in Bangkok and in social circles of mostly *farang*, Khao was able to navigate the fire scene more easily than others. For Khao, the city park is a space in which she felt comfortable experimenting with different gendered surfaces, in terms of dress and dance aesthetics. Most of her fire dance engagement was at the park with travelers and in other countries as a tourist; Khao did not perform on the beaches, a context that might shift how her body would be interpreted. For her, it is strictly a hobby that has afforded her friends and an enjoyable movement practice that she can travel with. Still, however, the social etiquette concerning femininity, even in the park, is one that Khao must navigate alongside her own desires to embody a cosmopolitan *phu chai* style. Because of her urban positioning, and her immersion in *farang* worlds in Bangkok, unlike many Thai women I know, Khao regularly jammed and met up with male fire spinners, many of them tourists, without her boyfriend present. In fact, I rarely saw her with women. It is, however, difficult to say if Khao would have ever learned if it had not been for her *farang* partner, partly because of the social rules surrounding Thai female respectability and her own feelings that the island style was not for women. Khao had access to an independence and a lifestyle that were different from normalized social standards. As Khao herself stated, she was mostly around men and thus embodied a surface at the park that was her own mix of a style, one that had room for both fast tricks and graceful movements.

Dao

Dao, a center member discussed in chapter 3, started fire dancing through her Thai boyfriend. Out of each of the three Thai women I worked with, Dao was the most conservative and in line with idealized forms of Thai femininity. For instance, it was incredibly rare for her to be in public without her boyfriend. If he had to be away for a few days from the fire art center, someone would be given the role of a "big brother" to pick her up on the *motocy* and make sure she got home safely each night, as she did not drive. Dao did not drink, although on a few occasions I did see her smoke, something not considered acceptable for women. She dressed quite modestly during the days, although she wore more revealing clothing during performances, such as belly tops, tank tops, and short shorts. Dao was very soft-spoken and almost shy, which was different from how I perceived Khao and Kat. I also got the impression that Dao's family was more conservative; they did not accept her career move from being a teacher to a fire dancer.

Dao had studied dance growing up but was forced to stop and focus on university. While at university, her boyfriend had been doing *poi* in the park close by. She joined and found that *poi* fulfilled her desire to move, but it wasn't until she learned hoop that her passion for dance was reignited. Song, Dao's boyfriend, was quite advanced and had a background in martial arts. On a trip to Koh Samui, they went to the center, and Nah asked Song to come and join the team. His parents, unlike Dao's, were accepting of his decision to pursue fire art as a career choice. Dao stayed in Bangkok after university and got a teaching position. She soon met Khao, who helped her find a female *farang* hoop teacher. Eventually, Dao was asked to join the center in Koh Samui, and she left her teaching position and became fire artist.

In an interview with her and Song, Dao told me that this was not a typical job for women in Thai society and that this was likely the reason there were not more female dancers:

> DAO: For women, they do fire art as a hobby but not for a job.
>
> SONG: Maybe it's too manly.
>
> DAO: Or I think it might be that because for women, if they do this as a job, it's not stable. Like, in Thai society my money goes back to my family. They want me to have a stable job. I think in Thailand females kind of think like that. You get money every month, but freelance jobs like this is not like that, and it involves fire. It's dangerous.
>
> SONG: And if you are female [doing fire art], you are very outstanding because the way you do it is totally different. The movement of the woman [demonstrates graceful and slow body movements], people like to look. Maybe it's only in Thailand where it is few women but worldwide I see so many women who do this—hoopers, jugglers, *poi* spinners.
>
> AUTHOR: What did you mean about it being manly?
>
> SONG: The tools [equipment]. The way that you spin and your posture. You need power. It looks masculine like that, but women *should* do something like this.

DAO: I think if it's masculine stuff and women start to practice, maybe they think it's not for them.

Like Khao, Song and Dao also expressed female movement as being graceful and slow, while the powerful aesthetic of spinning sticks and *poi*, like they do at the beach bars, was considered to be a male practice. Dao typically performed with hoop or fire fan, two pieces of equipment that I have rarely seen men use and that naturally invite more elegant movements. Dao also communicated how she took a different path than many Thai women by choosing an unstable job. In speaking about her family obligations, Dao referenced the role for Thai female children, which is to support their parents as they grow older. While boys are expected to ordain as monks to transfer karmic merit to their parents and re-pay their debt for raising them, women repay this debt financially and by tak-ing care of the home. Dao was not able to participate in this role. The moral re-lationships and economies, so important in Thai social relations, were broken when Dao chose a less stable job.

Like Khao and Kat, Dao also felt different from the Thai women around her. She stated,

> When I am looking on my Facebook newsfeed, many of my friends are working in Bangkok. I know about their life, and I know about my life and they are so different. A few months ago, one of our friends who works in Bangkok came here to visit us and be a tourist on Koh Samui. And she had an opportunity to see our performance and everything, and she felt like it was so much fun and that time was flying so fast. She wanted to stay on Koh Samui. And she said that what I am doing right now is so great. She had fun and enjoyed this life so much more than her own life.

Dao expressed how she was happy with her choice to pursue something differ-ent and was enjoying her life more so than her friends. She nonetheless recog-nized her unconventional role. In other conversations, Dao said that doing fire art, and being the only female at the center, made her feel important and spe-cial, despite how she might be viewed by her parents. She explained, "I feel impor-tant in a way I never felt before. I'm not close with my parents. They discouraged me from dancing. Now when I love something, I don't want to tell them. They don't know what I truly am." While Dao struggled with the relationship she had with her parents, she always expressed to me that she was thankful for all they had done for her and that she understood their reservations as they desired the best life possible for her.

For Dao, learning hoop and expressing herself in the way fire art allowed be-came a transformational experience that shifted how she felt in society and in her own body. When I asked on another occasion what she meant by feeling more important, she stated,

> Ya, important and beautiful. Before, I worked as a teacher. A teacher is important to students. I felt a little bit like that, but important in like another way, in my career. I'm a teacher. I'm important to students. My job was that I have to teach. It's more like work and career. In fire dance or hula dancing, it's more me. I don't feel that I am working, but I play, I dance. It's important, but in a different way. This is dancing and when I was a teacher, I worked.

> AUTHOR: I saw the biography you wrote, and you said that the circle [hoop] makes you a "special woman."
>
> DAO: Yes hahaha! Special in this case is not ordinary. You're not somebody else, you're you, but a better version—a more beautiful version. Like, if I didn't try that circle, I wouldn't even know what I am hiding. I'd never know what I am capable of. Like why did I learn so fast? Why did I click with this circle, you know? And even sometimes when I perform, when it comes out, I don't even know how I made it that way. Like I don't even know how it comes out like that, so I learn that it is my nature.
>
> AUTHOR: Does the hoop help to bring it out more than *poi* or other dancing?
>
> DAO: Yes. It's more than that because it's not particularly dancing that has the moves and all this stuff. I just flow with the hoop, flow with the music. Everything comes out naturally and that is my style. That is me. I feel myself more beautiful.

While Dao's life has been quite different from that of other Thai female dancers who have typically been in *farang* social circles, prior to learning fire art, she embodied and in many ways still embodies proper Thai femininity of the national ideal. However, she communicated that fire art brings out another special part of herself, one she feels is more beautiful—a passionate underpinning to a different surface that is unknown by her parents and would have remained hidden even to her. I recall watching Dao dance and seeing this powerful and distinct transformation, more so than in any other dancers I saw. I commented on this many times to Dao, which we would giggle about as I tried to enact and perform such a transformed surface as I practiced hoop with her; Dao's movements would lengthen, her eyes would brighten, and she would move incredibly gracefully, but almost flirtatiously. She herself characterized this transformation as a time when she could be "more feminine and sexy." Indeed, she often wore makeup and more revealing costuming in the context of performance, a surface that was only brought out with her hoop. For Dao, the hoop is a way in which she could embody what she refers to as the "special" and "not ordinary" woman in the context of societal gender roles. Being a fire dancer allowed Dao to experiment with new modalities of feminine labor, expression, and behavior, while it also supported the emergence of new surfaces in spaces of performance.

Dao, however, much like Kat, rarely performed at the beach bars. Rather, Dao performed almost exclusively at high-end hotels, which mitigates the stigma surrounding fire dance—a strategy Kat refers to above as "going corporate." In chapter 3, Dao also commented on how the beach shows are not as artistic as those at the hotels. The context of the hotel, associated with luxury art, was a more acceptable place for Dao to experiment with these different surfaces, rather than on the beach or the center that had mostly men and where she dressed and behaved conservatively. It was only in these luxury performance contexts that I saw Dao costume herself with revealing clothing, put on makeup, and move in "feminine" and "sexy" ways, as the special woman.

Celine

It is not only Thai women who felt like their dancing clashed with social mores. For Celine, a *farang* fire dancer originally from France who had been teaching in Bangkok for over seven years, doing fire art posed social problems. Celine had performed at very elite parties and hotels in Bangkok. She began by dancing for very little money, but after a year she could make more than what a beach dancer would for an entire night for just a twenty-minute set. Celine had learned flow art on the beaches in France when it first started becoming popular in the early 2000s, and she was quite advanced. I had met Celine in Myanmar in 2011 and learned that she was a founding member of the Bangkok group that Khao was in charge of, but Celine rarely danced when I visited her in 2016.

Interestingly, in the same way that Kat felt the Thai prostitute haunted her surface, Celine's gender and sexuality were haunted by what she refers to as the "the go-go," a figure who dances sexually for the pleasure of men. She explained, "I practiced fire dance and went home and told my Mom I was a performer in Bangkok, but she said she did not raise a go-go dancer. Why does my skirt take away my skill? This is why I don't like feminism; you can't be beautiful and intelligent at the same time." Often when performing, female fire artists wear few clothes, like men, and while this may be aesthetically appealing to the audience, it is first and foremost a safety measure; having loose clothing that can catch on fire is dangerous. She related how at one show, where she arrived wearing a mini-skirt and small shirt, she was asked to change because they did not want her to look like a "sexy dancer." "I'm not a go-go dancer!" Celine exclaimed in anger over this assumption. While it is unclear if Celine was referring to the iconic figure of the Thai bar-girl, I wonder if her mother's association of performance in Thailand with sexuality may have contributed to her disapproval.

Celine struggled with this figure for much of our interview and expressed her ambivalence about not being viewed as a skilled artist, as someone who is intelligent and serious but who also might be physically attractive. Some of these assumptions were, Celine thought, produced through being viewed as a sort of background décor at events rather than as a valued artist. She related, like Kat, how at events she felt like she was just part of the visual pleasure; this is different from how male fire dancers expressed their roles as affective laborers fully engaged with the audience and more than just visual decoration, although they, too, were aware of how their physical appearance was important. These were issues, however, that extended beyond the critiques of her mother and reverberated with what she felt was Thai society's complicated relationship with dance:

> Here, not only fire dancers, but any dancer is background décor. I've never seen anyone here paid for a dance performance on its own, except if it's a ballet from somewhere else and at the convention center. But apart from that, Thai or *farang*, in parties or events, we are just background. Even very good dancers are being paid nothing. And if they are Thai, it's even harder. Because when you are a *farang*, people might think, "Ok we're getting a *farang* so for the price we are going to consider this as a show." They take the Thai people, and they consider them like nothing, like, "You're a dancer, ya? You can move your ass." No, it's not only this. Like seven years of dance school and like fifteen years of practice and they are like, "Who cares. You are a hooker!" You are considered as a hooker if you are a dancer in Thailand. Unless you work for a ballet company in Thailand, you're a hooker. It's not recognized, not credited whatsoever.

The social limitations around dance in Thailand that Celine describes above are a phenomenon that I have also encountered. And, as Dao discussed, dancing was not an approved career choice, no matter what the genre. While for Dao this had to do with her responsibilities as a Thai women, dance is somewhat linked with prostitution in Thailand, and there is ambivalence toward dance unless it is a classical style. Given that many sex venues feature women dancing, there is a false connection here that is difficult to undo. I had never heard it articulated in this overt way but have felt the unstated social discomfort that emerges for women who dance in popular styles. This association and discomfort were so strong for Celine that she did not even tell her Thai boss or people where she worked that she was a fire artist. Unlike Thai women, however, Celine did not struggle with social obligations that dictate her role in the family or within Thai nationalist constructions of appropriate femininity. Rather, Celine struggled with her *farang* subjectivity.

What Celine also references above is the desire for *farang* performers, and this privileging of *farang* is not only for their idealized beauty aesthetics but for the cosmopolitan appeal that these performances can be sold through. As stated previously, Thailand has a complicated relationship with *farang*, who are at once reviled and desired. The cosmopolitan appeal, however, is something some Thais seek, and particularly hotels and events catering to tourists, to portray a modern persona (*samai mai*). Khao's discussion of city style, discussed earlier, engages with this desire to be *samai mai*. Despite how this privileging offered Celine better performance opportunities, she struggled with this positioning and stated, "You are never really integrated here. No. Never. Even if you speak Thai perfectly, and I do speak Thai quite well now, even then you will be the *farang* like, "You're a white face." This complex social desire and exclusion are another reason she felt that her art was not taken seriously and viewed as visual pleasure only. Mitigating this devalued artistic positioning and searching for what she felt were more appreciative audiences, however, was complicated for Celine.

> AUTHOR: So, you feel just part of the visual?
>
> CELINE: Yes, unless you do private parties. You are there because you are a sexy lady and there are going to be fifteen men having an expensive dinner and they want a private show having a sexy chick dancing in front of them.
>
> AUTHOR: Do you have to mingle with them after?
>
> CELINE: I did some private shows but no, I didn't mingle. I always refused to. I specified it before. I'm not a go-go dancer. And this is maybe a bit racist, and not something I've done, but one of my friends used to do shows for very rich Thai men that basically were just so happy to have a foreign dancer doing sexy moves in front of them. That is all. She's American. She's not very technical and she doesn't care about improving her technique because she is so beautiful and so graceful, and she absolutely knows that is why she was hired for most of the jobs. And I find it a bit horrible, to be honest, to have a bunch of Thai men like looking at her and being like, "Ya, she is sexy."

Celine desired to be viewed as differentiated from a go-go dancer and the excessively sexual *farang*. While she had privileges and flexibility not afforded to Thai women, it was clear that the sexualization of dance in Thailand, and the constructions of *farang* femininities, also deeply affected her life and possibilities to perform. While Kat appealed to her corporate surface to mitigate these associations, Celine attempted to demonstrate her technical abilities as a way to be viewed as a performer and a female who is "beautiful and intelligent at the same time" but she ultimately decided that leaving the industry was the better option.

Tiffany: The Author's Story

In the discussions above, we see that female performers seek to distance themselves from sexualized figures who remain in the background of their desired surfaces. Like Celine, I had a complicated relationship with how *farang* femininities and sexuality are constructed in Thailand and particularly in tourist areas that render *farang* as overly sexual. As I tried to shape my surface as that of a researcher, these associations lurked at the edges of my gender and sexuality in certain contexts. Yet at other times, when I sought to actually embody *farang* tourist femininity, in an effort to fit in at a particular bar, my surface was not able to produce the required aesthetics. Below, I present my experiences on Koh Phi Phi of my failures at *kalatesa* and crafting surfaces in the field.

I found myself almost embodying the knowledge of *kalatesa* naturally on Phi Phi, although never perfectly. Having lived in a conservative Thai neighborhood on the outskirts of Bangkok for three years, I had learned when and where I could wear tank tops, skirts, and makeup, drink beer, or have a partner come to my home. I became adept at picking up on small social cues, so common in Thailand, such as gestures and different smiles, which indirectly help one to shape one's social behaviors. On Phi Phi, I immediately intuited that the management of my surface was important in order for me to gain the trust of inhabitants. How I had to dress, interact, do my hair, consume beverages, move, and gesture was different on each side of the island. Gaining any amount of trust on Loh Dalum, the party beach, required a *farang* to have *farang*-style social capital, which meant a physically attractive body, with little clothing, and a flirty attitude with servers and other tourists. Gaining access to fire dancers on this side, outside of the beach parties, was almost impossible for me. Alexa, a *farang* bar manager, introduced me to a Burmese dancer and said that I wanted to learn and talk, but he replied cheekily in front of his team that I was not attractive enough. Being a good ten years older than most on Loh Dalum, I felt that I was always out of time and place. The only way to access dancers was through partying into the early mornings, which I did a few times during fieldwork. I was eventually asked to work at one bar, but I declined. I was not sure that my body could handle the nightly alcohol consumption that appeared to be mandatory if one were a par-tying *farang* worker. On Loh Dalum, I needed to embrace and perform the fig-ure of the sexualized *farang*, but I could never quite do it properly.

Because of these associations on Loh Dalum, I knew that spending too much time on that side could disrupt the relationships I was forming with Nam and his team of dancers on Ton Sai who often spoke disparagingly about tourists, *farang* workers, and dancers on Loh Dalum. Nam once said, "I meet many girls in the day. They say they are good girls and then I go there [the other side] and see them at night and they are like crazy [he motions dancing]." Nam, who used to work on the other side, also told me during this conversation that he knows everything that happens on the island, and I wondered whether he knew that I sometimes partied with some of the Burmese dancers at the bars lining the beach. I spent most of my afternoons at the quiet bar where Nam and his team worked practicing *poi* for a couple of hours. I dressed very modestly, with covered shoul-ders, longer shorts or pants, no makeup, and toned-down jewelry. While Plaa, the guesthouse owner where I stayed, told me I didn't have to obey the dress codes of Thai women, such as covering one's shoulders, I wanted to make the effort at the bar where Nam performed, particularly among the Muslim women who covered. Over time, and after taking lessons with one of the dancers, Kel, I started chatting with the team more informally, and they would share insights about fire dancing. Each afternoon, around 3:00 p.m., I would make my way down, buy a Diet Coke, and play *poi* on the quiet beach under the large frangi-pani tree. The guys would emerge and slowly start to prepare the sand stage for the night's performance. Shoveling and chatting, smoking, and drinking tea to-gether outside the gaze of tourists was a daily ritual for the fire dancers that I came to know well. After, they would wander to the local market to buy food and eat together. One of the dancers, Sanit, and his wife would eat together daily at this time. About halfway through the summer, Kel's wife came to stay with him on Phi Phi with their young son, and they, too, would eat together. I came to see this as family time at the bar when staff and their partners shared food and time outside the life of tourism. I tried to disturb them as little as possible during these times. However, this was one of the only times that the dancers were available to chat, and they encouraged me to come at this time.

My daily routine changed when Kel's wife, who had just had a baby, came to join him in August. She was very kind as he introduced me the first time as his student but was quite ambivalent about my presence as the days went on. There were more Thai women at the bar in the afternoons following her arrival, and none of them would even look at me. I was used to this dynamic with Sanit and his wife, as they did not really interact with me much, but this was different, and an indirect signal of nonacceptance that was palpable. It was awkward, but I would go out to my tree and practice as usual, sip my Diet Coke, and listen to the music, hoping that they would see me differently from other *farang* tourists. After a week or so, Kel also stopped interacting with me. I said hello one day when I walked in, and the discomfort on his face and through his body further confirmed my feelings as he walked past and ignored me. He never stopped building the stage to show me tricks anymore, as he usually did, and our lessons ended. I noticed that even Pon, a server who would regularly chat with me in the afternoons, was much less engaged when the wives and other Thai women were around. People, in turn, became increasingly interested in my relationship status. I always said I was married; I was actually engaged, although that is not really understood. But that my partner was not there with me left doubt in many people's mind. Pon, for instance, asked a few times, and Chew, the dancer who never spoke with me, inquired through Neo if I had a "*faen* Thai," a Thai boyfriend. I had moved from *farang* tourist to researcher to friend and then to outsider in a complicated and at times painful playing out of gender, sexuality, and global relations.

A final culminating moment of shame assured me that my presence, and my doing of gender and sexuality, was not working as I had hoped. In front of the Thai women, Pon began questioning me about what I did in the evenings, loud enough so that others could hear. I said I mostly went to bed early, worked, and wrote about what I had learned during the day. "You need some time to take it easy," she said, and that was an indirect way of drawing attention to my daily presence in the afternoons at the bar. Yes, I agreed, and I told her that my husband was coming in a week for a vacation. She responded, "Oh, you have a boyfriend!?" This confused me, because we had talked about my partner many times. Yes, I assured her. "Is he Thai?" asked Pon with a stern look. "No," I responded. "Ok. I was worrying that you have a Thai boyfriend. I hope he is not Thai." Pon walked away toward the other women, who had all stopped to listen to the interaction, and left me in my shame. While the magnitude of this encounter is difficult to communicate, this was a clear way for Pon to let me know that my presence, and doing of gender and sexuality, was being questioned. Direct critique is not socially acceptable in Thailand, but this was a way for Pon to "poke" at me, as Kat said of these indirect forms of criticism when I asked her about what I could have done better in this situation. I interpret Pon's remarks as indicating that a Thai boyfriend would not appreciate how I was interacting with men. I had been breaking the social rules surrounding gender, sexuality, space, and time at the bar on Ton Sai.

In my knowledge of *kalatesa*, I forgot to consider the change that other people bring to the operation of gender and sexuality in a space. Any one person who enters the space changes the relations and how one must act and embody gender. The Thai women, and particularly Kel's wife, changed the relations. I was breaking social codes that concerned how men and women interact. I had failed to regard the gender segregation at the bar during the day. As I thought back, the only men and women who interacted were relatives or couples. Otherwise, the men built the stage and the women sat at the table together. I, quite boldly, chatted and practiced with the men. It seemed that there were only certain times a *farang* woman should be interacting with dancers, and that was during the evening fire shows where social interaction is more of a performance. My body was disruptive in this space, which was coupled with the construction of *farang* female sexuality as uninhibited, inappropriate, and overt. My affiliation with a prestigious university, my role as a student, my upcoming marriage, my modest dress, and my Thai language skills were not enough here in the afternoons. I decided to stop going after that day because I felt that my presence was upsetting others. As a PhD student at that time intent on collecting data, I sat with the fear that perhaps I would leave Phi Phi with nothing after I had invested so much time. Yet something came unexpectedly from this encounter, and that is how I was able to develop a closer relationship with Nam.

After this incident, Nam suggested that his shop was the best place for us to talk about fire dance. While my presence there likely drew some suspicion, he was always very quick to explain to his friends who stopped by that I was interviewing him about fire dance. Nam approached the awkward subject of my absence at the bar one day. He said that the dancers wanted me to come to the bar but that they could not talk to me "because they are tired." Nam was trying to communicate the dynamics in a way that wouldn't embarrass me or make me lose face. They wanted to talk to me, he said, but sometimes they cannot because of certain people who are around. They "cannot make friends with tourists" and "sometimes we don't talk because we cannot," Nam explained. I nodded that I understood and asked why they couldn't make friends, and he said that the owner doesn't like them to. I wondered if this had to do with maintaining the image of the bar as different from the other side where *farang* women and fire dancers often hung out together. I could sense Nam was struggling with this, and he said that his friends asked him to relate that they wanted to talk to me "because you are a good person and you stay here for a long time," but they couldn't. The relations of time, space, and bodies would not allow my body to spend time with the team at the bar, but the proper context aligned at Nam's shop, a space outside the view of others, and with no females present, to make our engagements possible.

While we all had vastly different life experiences, privileges, knowledges, and figures that disturbed our desired surfaces, there are similarities that can be gleaned in looking at the experiences of diverse women in the Thai fire dance scene. We all somehow found ourselves out of time and place (*phit kalatesa*) and had to use a variety of means to be taken seriously and be understood as we wished. We each, differently, tried to distance ourselves from haunting presences: for Kat, the prostitute; for Celine, the go-go dancer; for Khao, the soft Asian *phu ying*; for myself, the *farang* tourist; and for Dao, the ordinary Thai woman. All of us also attempted to shift our surfaces and how they were interpreted through fire dance in certain spaces, whether that be stylistically, technically, through changing the audiences one performs for, or by commercializing one's art.

There are, however, also striking differences in our experiences. Celine and I had much more freedom, and less consequences, in trying out different surfaces. While we do not have the same social obligations or the same ideals to live up to, we also were not heavily reliant on income from this movement practice and thus had more room for experimentation. In turn, our outward *farang* aesthetics and subjectivities assisted us in being able to access different spaces in ways that unaccompanied Thai females likely could not. *Farang* women, while not having to negotiate national ideologies, must work within a system that views *farang* sexuality as potentially corrupting, even while our bodies are privileged through beauty hierarchies. In considering the insights and experiences of the Thai women featured here, however, we must remember that they, too, are involved in *farang* worlds and have access to cosmopolitan social capital that is not afforded to other Thais, even though these same associations can cause tensions in their lives.

The insights shared here, particularly surrounding the unruly sexuality that is ascribed to females who labor through dance, speak to the ways in which capitalism has reconfigured the roles of female entertainers, particularly in Asia (Maciszewski 2006; Pilzer 2006; Qureshi 2006; Srinivasan 1985). Joshua Pilzer's (2006) work with Korean *gisaeng* performers, for example, demonstrates how the movement and intensification of capitalist development are coupled with changing notions of morality, which has profoundly affected traditions of female entertainers across Asia. The development of modern sex-entertainment industries has created stigma around previously acceptable and respectable forms of female performance labor. As noted above, changes to economic policy and gendered nationalism in Thailand are intertwined with female gender and sexual surfaces. While it is beyond the scope of this research, we must think about what types of Thai female professional performers may have precluded the iconic Thai bar girls—stigmatized by not embodying the respectable femininity of neoliberal Thai nationalism—and how these histories and the erasures of particular bodies have also shaped the male-dominated fire dance world.

While tourism has provided opportunities for new types of artistic labor, there are considerable social consequences for taking these roles. Men seek distance from the figure of the beach boy and legitimize their craft through discussions of the various abilities and moralities an artist must have. Much like the male dancers who shared their experiences and maneuvers around their eroticization, women must also mitigate the social deviancy associated with fire dance and beach contexts. Appealing to particular visions of what constitutes art or artistic morality can be found throughout the conversations with men. Thai women, however, discuss the ways in which they already feel different from the national constructions and social mores of ideal public Thai femininity and how fire dance has offered opportunities to experiment with different surfaces. While women did not speak about certain moralities they have as dancers, they did not dance at the beach bars where men do but rather in high-end hotels, a different context. These venues have a certain respectability and cosmopolitan appeal attached to them, which helps to mitigate the unruliness that gets ascribed to dancing bodies. These spaces, however, invoke white Eurocentric aesthetics of what constitutes artistry and present further insight into the complexity of contexts such as Thailand and ongoing processes of colonialism that set standards on which bodies, embodiments, and surfaces are appropriate in particular spaces and times.

FEELING TOGETHER

AUTHOR: Why will some Thai fire dancers not work with the Burmese?
NAH: It's a culture thing. From what I know, and I don't know if it's true, a long time ago Burma's king changed, and when they changed their king they had to prove their power by attacking Thailand because Thailand is very healthy with the nature and food and everything. So, we are kind of rich. With the Buddhists it's the same like Christians—they put all the money inside the temples; in Thailand we put the gold inside the statues and we cover them with clay. And the new Burmese king and army came to Ayutthaya [former capital] to chop the heads off of statues, burn the city, and take the gold back to their country. We learn this history at school almost every year. Of course, when we were young, we feel angry, but if you go to speak with the Burmese now, they don't even know about it. Before I opened the center, Zaw left to go back to Burma, but I asked him to come back to join the team. I brought him to come and work with me in Ayutthaya, the city Burma burned down. I have a picture of us. Pan saw everything. There were two-hundred performers performing the war between Thailand and Burma [annual historical performance of the fall of Ayutthaya]. And me—Thai, and Zaw—Burmese, we spin fire behind the performance. He was like, "What happened?!" So, I said Burma came and burned it. And he cried. Ya, he was crying, and we made a show together.

This story, widely shared and taught in Thailand, tells of when the old Siamese capital, Ayutthaya, was taken by Burma in 1569 and held for thirty-four years before it was won back by Siam. In 1767 the Burmese came back and burned Ayutthaya, stole all the valuables, and left it in ruins. This event continues to fuel constructions of the Burmese as aggressive and barbaric and is a way in which Thailand reinforces its geopolitical boundaries (Chongkittavorn 2001; Johnson 2013; Winichakul 1994). Nah shared the story above as evidence of the cross-cultural relationships that form through fire dance, an art form that developed from unexpected relationships between Thais and tourists. Fire dancing at the reenactment rewrote these politics as Nah danced alongside Zaw, a Burmese dancer, and they both learned about the inconsistencies of history and the forces that erect and destabilize divides.

I often came back to this story while writing to reflect on the ways hopefulness, friendship, and solidarity are complexly situated within, and crystallize through, tourism industries. Tourism organizes bodies in unusual and unlikely ways. For some fire artists, because they dance, work, and share together, new and somewhat unimaginable bonds form. Without the capitalist logics of accumulation and expansion, fire dance may not have entered this economy, and Burmese and Thai migrant laborers may not have found themselves working as dancers and undergoing transformations that they consider important. These transformations are not only symbolic but also material. While wider Thai society positions fire dancers as invaluable beach laborers, through fire dance, young people from disadvantaged areas in Thailand and Myanmar create new lives and opportunities that the vast majority of society does not have—many fire dancers are transnationally connected, speak multiple languages, travel all over the country and abroad, and are connected in rich communities of support, and the highest-paid dancers make generous salaries. In some ways, they gain more power than those who marginalize them. As Som believes, it is not only hard work that has transformed his life but an underlying magic that generated the serendipitous connections that led him to success. For Nam, it was a push to strive forward and the felt connection with particular figures and objects that motivated him to keep going. This is the force of affect (Rosaldo 1989).

In the months following fieldwork, I worked with fire dancers over social media on analysis. Our conversations often surrounded how to phrase the various ways that affect gets discussed. Dao advised that the word *phalang* (energy) encapsulated much of what drives fire dancers. She explained, "This word in Thai is kind of broad. It can mean force, as well. And this *phalang* inspires us to create our own art and do what makes us happy." All fire dancers referenced affect in one way or another—vibes, *phalang*, feeling, spirits, magic, energy—and gave name to it. These articulations demonstrate the culturally variable ways that affect is known. For fire dancers, affects are preconscious intensities as well as named emotional elements. These perspectives bridge what are considered distinct approaches in affect studies.

The descriptions dancers use highlight an underlying resonance and a bodily feeling, but they are invoked to describe what affect does. Energy is the connective glue of relationships, the thrust of spirits and magic to imagine a world otherwise, and a tool to create moralities and reimagine fire dancer subjectivities. Affect forges the intercultural intimacy of sharing (*baeng pan*), the affinitive labor of making new lives on the beaches (Kojima 2016), and the secret histories ignited through shared goals (*chut mung mai*). The energies of fire dance offer corporeal transformations from poor beach boys into "special humans" (*manut*) and support experimentations with new surfaces (Van Esterik 2000).

There are messy dissonances in this affective economy. The same energies that are shared to build communities and a moral artistry also generate income. Giving tourists energies makes them feel like they want to give money, dancers explain. Affect draws in tourists so they stay at the beach bars and continue to push the economy forward. While the industry is remarkable for the connections that can blur delineations among tourist/inhabitant, Thai/*farang*, and Thai/Burmese, affect also radically reinscribes divisions. Energies in the industry activate desires and the seductive rhythms of capitalism that can be wielded to reinvigorate boundaries of belonging.

Categories of social difference never fully disappear in fire dance worlds; normative boundaries around ethnonational affiliations, socioeconomic class, race, nationality, sexuality, and gender are enlivened at times. And yet identities are made changeable by energies that are not easily contained. The affective transfer among performers and tourists supports a relation that complicates binaries situating tourists and inhabitants as completely separate. Affect undoes the borders of bodies and invites connections and solidarities based on feeling. Selves and communities float through forms of cohesiveness, emerging from and falling back into wider assemblages. Affect highlights the ever-changing nature of connections among bodies. It destabilizes social divisions and offers potentials to understand identities and communities as fluidly negotiated, in line with Theravada Buddhist perspectives that center such dynamism.

Ethnomusicologist Beverley Diamond (2007) argues that the academic focus on identity instantiates a performative practice of searching for distinctive categories and patterns of difference. She suggests that we also examine how and through which mechanisms people both assert and transcend social divisions by considering "alliances" (2007). Alliances are abundant in this scene, and they are centered in corporeal engagements and sensations. They manifest through

affects that are felt and exchanged in performance and behind the scenes as dancers share time together in deep and meaningful ways. Alliances emerge not only
among people but also with objects, and across time and space: Nam's *chut mung
mai*, for instance, highlights his affective alliances with objects of nostalgia that
animate "secret" genealogies connecting him to *Indian Daeng* and Thai rastas.
The development of flow puts people in alliances with objects, with future selves,
and with all those who have shared with them in the development of their own
style. The social divisions that manifest through these alliances sometimes reverberate with entrenched constructions of social identities, but the assertion of
boundaries revolves more so around an ability to tap into the affective dimension
and feel the labor of dance as fulfilling a purpose beyond the market economy.

The worlds of fire dancers reveal what affect does but more importantly demonstrate what people *do with* affect. It is not only an underlying force pushing
and pulling people into states of feelings and connections; fire dancers work with
and manage energies to their own ends—for capital, friendships, community,
connections, and moralities; for moving people and being moved; and for dream-
ing and pursuing new lives. People activate the force of affect. Activations can
be as extreme as the whirlwind energies that dancers layer over DJ'd music
toward alcohol-fueled abandon at beach bars or as subtle as sharing food and
laughter with friends.

The importance of these quiet moments cannot go unnoticed. The mellow and
hushed affects of the everyday have far-reaching resonances: long, slow days
spent practicing in a park; a shared smile and joke that evolve into a friendship;
quick bursts of teaching through YouTube videos on the edges of bars; and chance
encounters among fire dancers and tourists that generate new lives and relations.
This is the affective work of "feeling together," as Pi Neung would say.

Feeling together implies connectivity in a physical sense; one might feel that
one's energy aligns with another person's, similar to how Nu described how we
could feel each other's moods as we sat next to each other. And it also describes
a sensation of intimate bonding. Fire dancers argue that affect opens space to
connect with and know people—how a person feels—more potently than through
cognitive assessment alone.

Affect is the most prominent element in how fire dancers grapple with their
labor and form communities, and this invites us to ask, what political possibilities are offered when people feel together? How does feeling together enliven social and political engagement? As they dance, and as they share time and their
perspectives on the issues and possibilities of touristic labor, feeling together becomes an avenue for political engagement. By resituating monetary exchange
as affective sharing, dancers reimagine the intersections of fire art and touristic
labor. This is how they experience the feeling of art, as Jes states. When labor is

considered part of a wider affective economy, a connective force becomes the central focus. The scene is a platform for Thais, tourists, and Burmese people to form bonds in an industry that benefits from tensions and divisions. Affect is employed to make fire dance a transformative political experience that is more than a means to economic survival. Political agency is manifested through the ephemeral affects of danced labor—the "liveness" (Srinivasan 2011). This liveness is not only consumed by tourist audiences; it is employed, experienced, and managed by all as a potent force of engagement in a context where political critique is not always possible.

While Thailand has long histories of protests and large-scale political movements, violent state interventions circulate in the public consciousness as reminders of the price agitators pay. Universalizing logics of agency centered in notions of free will gloss the multifaceted ways that people participate in political life in contexts where critique is constrained (Cassaniti 2015b). Julia Cassaniti points out that in Thailand agency is "oriented to particular kinds of emotional practices and religiously influenced ontological assumptions that work to create effects through the acceptance of change" (2015b, 179). This is an agency that is enacted through letting go (*ploy wang*) so that one can be more in control of one's own emotions. For example, people may tackle social issues through fostering calmness (*jai yen*) rather than through direct opposition or contestation. It is through *phalang* that fire dancers engage in politics, often changing and recreating their emotions, bodies, and histories to critique social issues and mediate the neoliberal capitalist industry in which their art is nested.

Fire dance energies allow for a reworking of the political through the body. The ephemera of moving bodies explodes out from limbs and toys, spinning off in fiery traces against the darkness for all to see. Sparks from fire *poi* become more than aesthetic pleasure; they are ephemeral forces that move power from the grips of regimes and into the hands of people (Cvetkovich 2003; Manalansan IV 2014; Muñoz 1996). The traces of light are manifestations of affect that dancers create and manage—a visualization of the ways in which emotion interfaces with politics. Aesthetics of moving bodies are correlated with specific energies, communicating new histories and challenging representations while also offering a bodily space to *ploy wang*. The aesthetic of slow flow is a challenge to capitalist logics, and it centers an ethos and a history of artistry and sharing. Dance aesthetics thus do not solely function as a visual spectacle for audiences—for fire dancers, they are "a series of tactics for living, not simply a strategy for moving" (Hamera 2007, 210).

Energies oscillate between the dominance of capitalism and normative structures of gender, sexuality, class, ethnicity, and morality and the intimacies that disrupt these same systems. This is the mess of affect. These dissonances do not foreclose potentials for connection, affinities, dreams, and solidarity. Rather, mess is the product of people working out the complexities of labor, art, and community in the tourism industry. The affects of fire dance are a site of continuous tension and release as ideas, people, desires, cultures, and capital collide, at times impeding each other and at other times moving smoothly along. This turbulent rhythm is echoed through bodies that move their way into relations with objects, such as *poi*, hoops, and staff.

Juggling, the movement practice that underpins fire dance, is a rhythmic act of controlled tension and a release. It is based on motions of subjugation through which dancing bodies are invited to experience moments of resistance, control, and liberation as they extend themselves into space. The bodies of fire dancers enact nightly renderings of control and expansion in tourist economies that are unpredictable and messy and yet also offer generative moments and intimacies. The fire-dancing body learns to work with this tension and to control and shape it into patterned rhythms and flows. Fire dance is a practice born from long histories of dissonant encounters that manifest in the body tensing and releasing, building, and resolving. These are not opposing forces; rather, they are mutually necessary in fire art.

Acknowledgments

Thank you to all the fire artists whom I had the great privilege of working with and who shared so much with me. I am grateful for the many teachers, travelers, friends, and *ajarns* (professors) in Thailand who supported this project. My mentors—Profs. David Murray, Penny Van Esterik, Alison Crosby, and Kenneth Little—have provided endless encouragement. They not only helped me to refine the ideas in this book and conduct fieldwork with a collaborative and fun spirit; they taught me to enjoy every step of the process.

This work has benefited from the advice and suggestions of the two anonymous reviewers, many colleagues and my family and friends. Special thank you to Profs. Julia Cassaniti, Martin Manalansan, and Alicia Turner for helping me push my ideas further. Thank you to my editor, Sarah Grossman, for believing in this project and supporting me in bringing it to life.

I acknowledge the support of the Social Sciences and Humanities Research Council of Canada and the Center of Excellence for Thai Music and Culture Research at Chulalongkorn University.

The photos were edited by Alex Felipe. The maps were drawn by Bill Nelson.

Notes

INTRODUCTION

1. There is no formal history of fire dance that details precisely when this art form arrived in Thailand. Oral histories suggest that the practice started around the same time as the famous full moon beach parties began at Paradise Bungalows in the mid-1980s on the island of Koh Phangan and started to become popular in the late 1990s and 2000s. This coincides with flow art's emerging popularity in Europe and North America.

2. *Poi* dance, a practice among the Maori in Aotearoa, has greatly influenced flow art. The word *poi* refers to both the dance and the object used—a ball attached to a rope (Condevaux 2009).

3. There is a significant Muslim minority in Thailand, particularly in the South, as well as Christians, Hindus, and Sikhs, among other religions. The majority of fire dancers I worked with were Theravada Buddhists.

4. *Chao le* (people from the sea) is a broad term that refers to distinct ethnic groups of nomadic maritime people who settled in the Andaman region. They are often referred to as Sea Gypsies or Sea People. See Coeli 2018.

5. While the country is referred to as both Myanmar and Burma, Myanmar is the official name, which was changed from Burma in 1989. When speaking about dancers, I refer to them as Burmese, as that is how they refer to themselves, but I refer to the country as Myanmar.

6. *Farang* is a word that describes a foreigner. It is most often applied to Caucasian people from countries in Europe, North America, and Australia, as well as countries such as Israel and Brazil, who form a large percentage of tourists and appear white. In 2019, however, I started to hear *farang* increasingly applied to Burmese workers and Chinese tourists. While it can be a friendly term, there is an underlying ambivalence when the word when is said in particular contexts.

7. Paul Ricoeur first coined the hermeneutics of suspicion (1970).

1. TRANSFORMING FIRE DANCE SURFACES

1. In Thailand, gender and sexuality are considered "as aspects of a single complex rather than as separate categories." The Thai word *phet* can refer to a broad range of phenomena including what is often categorized in English as: biological sex, gender, sexuality, and the act of sexual intercourse (Jackson and Cook 1999, 4). The Thai gender system is best understood as a nonbinary continuum with fluid and permeable boundaries which people can move into and out of through modes of self-presentation and behavior (Käng 2014; Morris 1994; Van Esterik 2000), although within the fluidity, there can certainly be moments of stasis (Costa and Matzner 2007; Hidalgo 2009).

2. The Korean Wave refers to the transnational spread of Korean popular culture among young people, starting in the 1990s across Southeast Asia and China (Bok-Rae 2015).

3. "Pi" in front of a Thai name indicates one's seniority.

3. FEELING ART AND THE LABOR OF SHARING

1. Pi Neung refers to flow art and fire dancing as "juggling," a term that was used less often but recognized by all fire artists. Juggling, the art of coordinating one's bodily movement with pieces of equipment in rhythmic patterns, underlies all descriptions I have heard of fire dance, despite the different names given to it (i.e., fire art, fire dance, and playing fire, etc.).

2. The notion of debt to one's teacher (*khru*) and the relationship between a student and a teacher in Thailand are very important. In Thai classical music, this relationship is one instilled with cosmic power, connections to ancestors, and the passing down of specialized knowledge in particular lineages. Each year there is a ceremony, *wai khru*, in which teachers are honored by students (Wong 2001).

3. A *wai* is the standard bowed greeting done by putting the two hands palm to palm in the middle of the chest. It is typically initiated first by those of lower social status as a form of respect.

4. THE AFFINITIVE LABOR OF FREEDOM

An earlier version of this chapter was published as Tiffany Pollock (2019), "Migration, Affinity and the Everyday Labour of Belonging among Young Burmese Men in Thailand," *Boyhood Studies: An Interdisciplinary Journal* 12 (2): 114–30, https://doi.org/10.3167/bhs.2019.120207.

1. Similar juxtapositions can be found in the Thai context where Pattana Kitiarsa (2013) discusses the monk and the muay thai fighter as a nexus of Thai masculinity. Despite their surface differences, both figures imprint discipline on the bodies of young men and, I would add, function through the ability to enact power over others and over the self.

6. STRIVING ON KOH PHI PHI

1. This is a reference to the Sea Gypsies (*chao le*) who were the original inhabitants of Koh Phi Phi.

2. Nam used *chon klum noi* to describe Sea Gypsies; it translates as "ethnic minority."

References

Ahmad, Tania. 2016. "Intolerants: Politics of the Ordinary in Karachi, Pakistan." In *Impulse to Act: A New Anthropology of Resistance and Social Justice*, edited by Othon Alexandrakis, 135–60. Bloomington: Indiana University Press.

Ahmed, Sara. 2004. *The Cultural Politics of Emotion*. New York: Routledge.

Alexandrakis, Othon. 2016. "Incidental Activism: Graffiti and Political Possibility in Athens, Greece." *Cultural Anthropology* 31 (2): 272–96.

Alexeyeff, Kalissa. 2009. *Dancing from the Heart: Movement, Gender, and Cook Islands Globalization*. Honolulu: University of Hawai'i Press.

Allerton, Catherine. 2009. "Introduction: Spiritual Landscapes of Southeast Asia." *Anthropological Forum* 19 (3): 235–51. https://doi.org/10.1080/00664670903278387.

Århem, Kaj. 2016. "Southeast Asian Animism in Context." In *Animism in Southeast Asia*, edited by Kaj Århem and Guido Sprenger, 3–30. London: Routledge. https://doi-org.ezproxy.library.yorku.ca/10.4324/9781315660288.

Barad, Karen. 2007. *Meeting the Universe Halfway: Quantum Physics and the Entanglement of Matter and Meaning*. Durham, NC: Duke University Press.

Batnitzky, Adina, Linda McDowell, and Sarah Dyer. 2009. "Flexible and Strategic Masculinities: The Working Lives and Gendered Identities of Male Migrants in London." *Journal of Ethnic and Migration Studies* 35 (8): 1275–93. https://doi.org/10.1080/13691830903123088.

Berlant, Lauren Gail. 2011. *Cruel Optimism*. Durham, NC: Duke University Press.

Boellstorff, Tom, and Johan Lindquist. 2004. "Bodies of Emotion: Rethinking Culture and Emotion through Southeast Asia." *Ethnos* 69 (4): 437–44. https://doi.org/10.1080/0014184042000302290.

Bok-Rae, Kim. 2015 "Past, Present and Future of Hallyu (Korean Wave)." *American International Journal of Contemporary Research* 5 (5): 154–60.

Boris, Eileen, and Rhacel Salazar Parreñas. 2010. *Intimate Labors: Cultures, Technologies, and the Politics of Care*. Stanford, CA: Stanford Social Sciences.

Bowie, Katherine A. 1998. "The Alchemy of Charity: Of Class and Buddhism in Northern Thailand." *American Anthropologist* 100 (2): 469–81. https://doi.org/10.1525/aa.1998.100.2.469.

Brennan, Denise. 2004. "Women Work, Men Sponge, and Everyone Gossips: Macho Men and Stigmatized/ing Women in a Sex Tourist Town." *Anthropological Quarterly* 77 (4): 705–33. https://doi.org/10.1353/anq.2004.0050.

Brennan, Teresa. 2004. *The Transmission of Affect*. Ithaca, NY: Cornell University Press.

Cabezas, Amalia L. 2009. *Economies of Desire: Sex Tourism in Cuba and the Dominican Republic*. Philadelphia: Temple University Press.

Cassaniti, Julia L. 2014. "Moralizing Emotion: A Breakdown in Thailand." *Anthropological Theory* 14 (3): 280–300. https://doi.org/10.1177/1463499614534551.

Cassaniti, Julia L. 2015a. "Intersubjective Affect and the Embodiment of Emotion: Feeling Supernatural in Thailand." *Anthropology of Consciousness* 26 (2): 132–42. https://doi.org/10.1111/anoc.12036.

Cassaniti, Julia L. 2015b. *Living Buddhism: Mind, Self, and Emotion in a Thai Community*. Ithaca, NY: Cornell University Press.

Cate, Sandra. 2003. *Making Merit, Making Art: A Thai Temple in Wimbledon*. Honolulu: University of Hawai'i Press.

Certeau, Michel de. 1984. *The Practice of Everyday Life*. Translated by Steven Rendall. Berkeley: University of California Press.

Charmaz, Kathy. 2006. *Constructing Grounded Theory: A Practical Guide through Qualitative Analysis*. London: Sage.

Chongkittavorn, Kavi. 2001. "Thai-Burma Relations." In *Challenge to Democratization in Myanmar: Perspectives in Multilateral and Bilateral Response*. Stockholm: International Institute for Democratic and Electoral Assistance.

Clough, Patricia T. 2008. "The Affective Turn: Political Economy, Biomedia and Bodies." *Theory, Culture & Society* 25 (1): 1–22. https://doi.org/10.1177/0263276407085156.

Coconuts Bangkok. 2017. "Twerk Irk: Prayuth Scolds Country Singer 'Lamyai' for Dirty Dance Moves." *Coconuts Bangkok*, July 13. https://coconuts.co/bangkok/news/twerk-irk-prayuth-scolds-country-singer-lamyai-dirty-dance-moves/.

Coeli, Barry. 2019. "Hierarchy and Diversity in Thailand's Changing Political Landscape." *Situations* 12 (1): 67–85

Cohen, Erik. 2008. *Explorations in Thai Tourism*. Bingley, UK: Emerald.

Condevaux, Aurélie. 2009 "Māori Culture on Stage: Authenticity and Identity in Tourist Interactions." *Anthropological Forum* 19 (2): 143–61. Routledge. https://doi.org/10.1080/00664670902980389.

Costa, LeeRay and Andrew Matzner. 2007. Male bodies, women's souls: Personal narratives of Thailand's transgender youth. New York: Haworth Press. Csikszentmihalyi, Mihaly. 1990. *Flow: The Psychology of Optimal Experience*. New York: Harper & Row.

Cvetkovich, Ann. 2003. *Archive of Feelings*. Vol. 2008. Durham, NC: Duke University Press.

Das, Veena. 2007. *Life and Words: Violence and the Descent into the Ordinary*. Berkeley: University of California Press.

Datta, Kavita, Cathy McIlwaine, Joanna Herbert, Yara Evans, John May, and Jane Wills. 2009. "Men on the Move: Narratives of Migration and Work among Low-Paid Migrant Men in London." *Social & Cultural Geography* 10 (8): 853–73. https://doi.org/10.1080/14649360903305809.

Deleuze, Gilles, and Félix Guattari. 1983. *Anti-Oedipus: Capitalism and Schizophrenia*. Minneapolis: University of Minnesota Press.

Deleuze, Gilles, and Félix Guattari. 1987. *A Thousand Plateaus: Capitalism and Schizophrenia*. Translated by B. Massumi. Minneapolis: University of Minnesota Press.

Desmond, Jane. 1999. *Staging Tourism: Bodies on Display from Waikiki to Sea World*. Chicago: University of Chicago Press.

Diamond, Beverley. 2007. "The Music of Modern Indigeneity: From Identity to Alliance Studies." *European Meetings in Ethnomusicology* 12 (22): 169–90.

Eng, David L. 2010. *The Feeling of Kinship: Queer Liberalism and the Racialization of Intimacy*. Durham, NC: Duke University Press.

Errington, Shelly. 1989. *Meaning and Power in a Southeast Asian Realm*. Princeton, NJ: Princeton University Press.

Finnegan, Dave, Todd Strong, and Allan Jacobs. 1987. *The Complete Juggler*. New York: Vintage Books.

Franko, Mark. 2002. *The Work of Dance: Labor, Movement and Identity in the 1930s*. Middletown, CT: Wesleyan University Press.

Fuhrmann, Arnika. 2009. "Nang Nak—Ghost Wife: Desire, Embodiment, and Buddhist Melancholia in a Contemporary Thai Ghost Film." *Discourse* 31 (3): 220–47. muse.jhu.edu/article/402308.

Gammeltoft, Tine M. 2016. "Silence as Response to Everyday Violence: Understanding Domination and Distress through the Lens of Fantasy." *Ethos* 44 (4): 427–47. https://doi.org/10.1111/etho.12140.

Geertz, Clifford. 1973. *The Interpretation of Cultures*. London: Fontana.

Gregg, Melissa, and Gregory J. Seigworth, eds. 2010. *The Affect Theory Reader*. Durham, NC: Duke University Press.

Guillou, Anne Yvonne. 2017. "Potent Places and Animism in Southeast Asia." *Asia Pacific Journal of Anthropology* 18 (5): 389–99. https://doi.org/10.1080/14442213.2017.1401324.

Hamera, Judith. 2007. *Dancing Communities: Performance, Difference, and Connection in the Global City*. Basingstoke, Hampshire: Palgrave Macmillan.

Hanks, Lucien M., Jr. 1962. "Merit and Power in the Thai Social Order." *American Anthropologist* 64: 1247–61. https://doi.org/10.1525/aa.1962.64.6.02a00080.

Hardt, Michael. 1999. "Affective Labor." *Boundary* 2 (26): 89–100. http://www.jstor.org/stable/303793.

Hardt, Michael, and Antonio Negri. 2000. *Empire*. Cambridge, MA: Harvard University Press.

Haritaworn, Jin. 2011. "Reckoning with Prostitutes: Performing Thai Femininity." In *New Femininities: Postfeminism, Neoliberalism and Subjectivity*, edited by Rosalind Gill and Christina Scharff, 215–29. Houndmills: Palgrave Macmillan. https://doi-org.ezproxy.library.yorku.ca/10.4324/9781315660288.

Harvey, David. 2001. *Spaces of Capital: Towards a Critical Geography*. New York: Routledge.

Henriques, Julian. 2010. "The Vibrations of Affect and Their Propagation on a Night Out on Kingston's Dancehall Scene." *Body and Society* 16: 57–89. https://doi.org/10.1177/1357034X09354768.

Henry, Rosita, Fiona Magowan, and David Murray. 2000. "Introduction." *Australian Journal of Anthropology* 11 (2): 253–60. https://doi.org/10.1111/j.1835-9310.2000.tb00041.x.

Herzfeld, Michael. 2002. "The Absent Presence: Discourses of Crypto-Colonialism." *South Atlantic Quarterly* 101 (4): 899–926. https://doi.org/10.1215/00382876-101-4-899.

Herzfeld, Michael. 2004. *The Body Impolitic: Artisans and Artifice in the Global Hierarchy of Value*. Chicago: University of Chicago Press.

Herzfeld, Michael. 2009. "The Culture Politics of Gesture: Reflections on the Embodiment of Ethnographic Practice." *Ethnography* 10 (2): 131–52. https://doi.org/10.1177/1466138109106299.

Hidalgo, Danielle Antoinette. "Expressions on a Dance Floor: Embodying Geographies of Genders and Sexualities in Bangkok Nightclubbing" (PhD Dissertation, University of California Santa Barbara, 2009.

High, Holly. 2014. *Fields of Desire: Poverty and Policy in Laos*. Singapore: NUS Press.

Hochschild, Arlie Russell. 2003. *The Managed Heart: Commercialization of Human Feeling*. 20th anniversary ed. Berkeley: University of California Press.

Howe, Cymene. 2016. "Negative Space: Unmovement and the Study of Activism When There Is No Action." In *A New Anthropology of Resistance and Social Justice*, edited by Othon Alexandrakis, 161–82. Bloomington: Indiana University Press. https://ebookcentral.proquest.com/lib/york/reader.action?docID=652478.

Ingold, Tim. 2011. *Being Alive: Essays on Movement, Knowledge and Description*. London: Routledge.

Jackson, Peter A. 2004. "The Thai Regime of Images." *Sojourn: Journal of Social Issues in Southeast Asia* 19 (2): 181–218. https://doi.org/10.1355/SJ19-2B.

Jackson, Peter A., and Nerida M. Cook, eds. 1999. *Genders and Sexualities in Modern Thailand*. Chiang Mai, Thailand: Silkworm Booksgreaves, D. J.

Johnson, Andrew. 2013. "Progress and Its Ruins: Ghosts, Migrants and the Uncanny in Thailand." *Cultural Anthropology* 28 (2): 299–319. https://doi.org/10.1111/cuan.12005.

Käng, Dredge Byung'chu. 2014. "Conceptualizing Thai Genderscapes: Transformation and Continuity in the Thai Sex/Gender System." In *Contemporary Socio-Cultural and Political Perspectives in Thailand*, edited by Pranee Liamputton, 409–29. Dordrecht, Netherlands: Springer.

Käng, Dredge Byung'chu. 2017. "Global K-pop Fandom: Challenging Dominant Narratives of Globalization, Spatial Hierarchies and Identity Formation." Paper presented at the annual meeting for the American Anthropological Association, Washington, DC, November 30.

Keeler, Ward. 1983. "Shame and Stage Fright in Java." *Ethos* 11 (3): 152–65. https://www.jstor.org/stable/639970.

Keeler, Ward. 2017. *The Traffic in Hierarchy: Masculinity and Its Others in Buddhist Burma*. Honolulu: University of Hawai'i Press.

Kisliuk, Michelle Robin. 1998. *Seize the Dance!: BaAka Musical Life and the Ethnography of Performance*. New York: Oxford University Press.

Kitiarsa. Pattana. 2013. "Of Men and Monks: The Boxing-Buddhism Nexus and the Production of National Manhood in Contemporary Thailand." *New Mandala Blog*, October 2. http://asiapacific.anu.edu.au/newmandala/2013/10/02/pattana-kitiarsaon-thai-boxing/.

Kojima, Dai. 2016. "The Hidden Palace: Everyday Practices and Performances of Affinitive Labour in Queer Japanese Migrant Lives." Paper presented at the Centre for Feminist Research Lecture Series, York University, Toronto, March 15.

Kontogeorgopoulos, Nick. 2016. "Tourism in Thailand: Growth, Diversification and Political Upheaval." In *The Routledge Handbook of Tourism in Asia*, edited by C. Michael Hall and Stephen J. Page, 149–63. New York: Routledge.

Kosofsky Sedgwick, Eve. 2003. *Touching Feeling: Affect, Pedagogy, Performativity*. Durham, NC: Duke University Press.

Kunst, Bojana. 2011. "Dance and Work: The Aesthetic and Political Potential of Dance." In *Emerging Bodies: The Performance of Worldmaking in Dance and Choreography*, edited by Gabriele Klein and Sandra Noeth, 47–60. New Brunswick, NJ: Transaction.

Lefebvre, Henri. 2004. *Rhythmanalysis: Space, Time, and Everyday Life*. London: Continuum.

Lewis, Ioan M. 1990. Preface to *Emotions of Culture: A Malay Perspective*, edited by Wazir Jahan Karim. Singapore: Oxford University Press.

Little, Kenneth. 2012. "Belize Blues." *Recherches Sémiotiques* 32 (1): 25–46. https://doi.org/10.7202/1027771ar.

Loos, Tamara Lynn. 2006. *Subject Siam: Family, Law, and Colonial Modernity in Thailand*. Ithaca, NY: Cornell University Press.

Love, Heather. 2009. *Feeling Backward: Loss and the Politics of Queer History*. Cambridge, MA: Harvard University Press.

Lutz, Catherine, and Geoffrey M. White. 1986. "The Anthropology of Emotions." *Annual Review of Anthropology* 15: 405–36. https://doi.org/10.1146/annurev.an.15.100186.002201.

Maciszewski, Amelia. 2006. "Tawa'if, Tourism, and Tales: The Problematics of Twenty-First Century Musical Patronage for North India's Courtesans." In *The Courtesan's Arts: Cross-Cultural Perspectives*, edited by Martha Feldman and Bonnie Gordon, 332–51. Oxford: Oxford University Press.

Mahmood, Saba. 2005. *Politics of Piety: The Islamic Revival and the Feminist Subject.* Princeton, NJ: Princeton University Press.

Malam, Linda. 2008a. "Bodies, Beaches and Bars: Negotiating Heterosexual Masculinity in Southern Thailand's Tourism Industry." *Gender, Place & Culture: A Journal of Feminist Geography* 15 (6): 581–594. Malam, Linda. 2008b. "Spatializing Thai Masculinities: Negotiating Dominance and Subordination in Southern Thailand." *Social & Cultural Geography* 9 (2): 135–50. https://doi.org/10.1080/1464936070 1856086.

Manalansan, Martin F., IV. 2005. "Migrancy, Modernity, Mobility: Quotidian Struggles and Queer Diasporic Intimacy." In *Queer Migrations: Sexuality, U.S. Citizenship, and Border Crossings,* edited by Eithne Luibhéid and Lionel Cantú Jr., 146–60. Minneapolis: University of Minnesota Press.

Manalansan, Martin F., IV. 2014. "The 'Stuff' of Archives: Mess, Migration, and Queer Lives." *Radical History Review* 120: 94–107. https://doi.org/10.1215/01636545 -2703742.

Manalansan, Martin F., IV. 2015. "The Messy Itineraries of Queerness." Theorizing the Contemporary, *Fieldsights,* July 21. https://culanth.org/fieldsights/the-messy -itineraries-of-queerness.

Manalansan, Martin F., IV. 2018 "Messing Up Sex: The Promises and Possibilities of Queer of Color Critique." *Sexualities* 21 (8): 1287–1290.

Manning, Erin. 2007. *Politics of Touch: Sense, Movement, Sovereignty.* Minneapolis: University of Minnesota Press.

Martin, Randy. 2011. "Between Intervention and Utopia: Dance Politics." In *Emerging Bodies: The Performance of Worldmaking in Dance and Choreography,* edited by Gabriele Klein and Sandra Noeth, 30–45. New Brunswick, NJ: Transaction.

Massey, Doreen B. 1994. *Space, Place and Gender.* Minneapolis: University of Minneapolis Press.

Massumi, Brian. 2002. *Parables for the Virtual: Movement, Affect, Sensation.* Durham, NC: Duke University Press.

McKay, Steven C. 2007. "Filipino Sea Men: Constructing Masculinities in an Ethnic Labor Niche." *Journal of Ethnic and Migration Studies* 33 (4): 617–33. https://doi .org/10.1080/13691830701265461.

Mitchell, James. 2011. "Kon Baan Diaokan or 'We're from the Same Village': Star/Fan Interaction in Thai Lukthung." *Perfect Beat* 12 (1): 69–89. https://doi.org/10.1558 /prbt.v12i1.69.

Morris, Rosalind C. 1994. "Three Sexes and Four Sexualities: Redressing the Discourses on Gender and Sexuality in Contemporary Thailand." *Positions: East Asia Culture Critique* 2 (1): 15–43. https://doi.org/10.1215/10679847-2-1-15.

Muñoz, José Esteban. 1996. "Ephemera as Evidence: Introductory Motes to Queer Acts." *Women & Performance* 8 (2): 5–16. https://doi.org/10.1080/07407709608571228.

Muñoz, José Esteban. 2006. "Feeling Brown, Feeling Down: Latina Affect, the Performativity of Race, and the Depressive Position." *Signs: Journal of Women in Culture and Society* 31 (3): 675–688. https://doi.org/10.1086/499080.

Nixon, Rob. 2011. *Slow Violence and the Environmentalism of the Poor.* Cambridge, MA: Harvard University Press.

Ockey, James. 1998. "Crime, Society and Politics in Thailand." In *Gangsters, Democracy, and the state in Southeast Asia,* edited by Carl A. Trocki, 15–35. Ithica: Southeast Asia Program Publications, Cornell University Press.

Osella, Filippo, and Caroline Osella. 2000. "Migration, Money and Masculinity in Kerala." *Journal of the Royal Anthropological Institute* 6: 111–13. https://doi.org/10.1111 /1467-9655.t01-1-00007.

Pholphirul, Piriya, and Pungpond Rukmnuaykit. 2010. "Economic Contribution of Migrant Workers to Thailand." *International Migration* 48 (5): 174–202. https://doi.org/10.1111/j.1468-2435.2009.00553.x.

Pilzer, Joshua D. 2006. "The Twentieth-Century 'Disappearance' of the Gisaeng during the Rise of Korea's Modern Sex-and-Entertainment Industry." In *The Courtesan Arts: Cross-Cultural Perspectives*, edited by Martha Feldman and Bonnie Gordon, 295–310. Oxford: Oxford University Press.

Polioudakis, Emanuel J. 1991. "Social Organization, Gender, and Adaptation in Southern Thailand." *Ethnology* 30 (1): 65–83. https://doi.org/10.2307/3773498.

Pollock, Tiffany. 2019. "Migration, Affinity and the Everyday Labour of Belonging among Young Burmese Men in Thailand." *Boyhood Studies: An Interdisciplinary Journal* 12 (2): 114–30. https://doi.org/10.3167/bhs.2019.120207.

Povinelli, Elizabeth A. 2002. "Notes on Gridlock: Genealogy, Intimacy, Sexuality." *Public Culture* 14 (1): 215–38. https://doi.org/10.1215/08992363-14-1-215.

Povinelli, Elizabeth A. 2011. *Economies of Abandonment: Social Belonging and Endurance in Late Liberalism*. Durham, NC: Duke University Press.

Qureshi, R. B. 2006. "Female Agency and Patrilineal Constraints: Situating Courtesans in Twentieth-Century India." In *The Courtesan Arts: Cross-Cultural Perspectives*, edited by Martha Feldman, and Bonnie Gordon, 312–31. Oxford: Oxford University Press.

Reuters in Bangkok. 2014. "Thai PM Apologizes for Bikini Warning after Britons' Murder." *The Guardian*, September 12. https://www.theguardian.com/world/2014/sep/18/thai-prime-minister-apologises-bikini-comments-murder.

Reynolds, Craig J., ed. 2002. *National Identity and Its Defenders: Thailand Today*. Chiang Mai: Silkworm Books.

Reynolds, Frank. 1990. "Ethics and Wealth in Theravada Buddhism: A Study in Comparative Religious Ethics." In *Ethics, Wealth, and Salvation: A Study of Buddhist Social Ethics*, edited by Russell A. Sizemore and Donald K. Swearer. Columbia: University of Southern Carolina Press.

Ricoeur, Paul. 1970. *Freud and Philosophy: An Essay on Interpretation*. New Haven, CT: Yale University Press.

Rosaldo, Michelle Zimbalist. 1980. *Knowledge and Passion: Ilongot Notions of Self and Social Life*. Cambridge: Cambridge University Press.

Rosaldo, Michelle Zimbalist. 1984. "Toward an Anthropology of Self and Feeling." In *Culture Theory: Essays on Mind, Self, and Emotion*, edited by Richard A. Sweder and Robert A. LeVine. Cambridge: Cambridge University Press.

Rosaldo, Renato. 1989. "Introduction: Grief and a Headhunter's Rage." In *Culture and Truth: The Remaking of Social Analysis*. Boston: Beacon.

Sakwit, Kunphatu. 2020. *Globalisation, Tourism and Simulacra: A Baudrillardian Study of Tourist Space in Thailand*. London: Routledge.

Saldanha, Arun. 2007. *Psychedelic White: Goa Trance and the Viscosity of Race*. Minneapolis: University of Minnesota Press.

Sawangchot, Viriya. 2013. "'Only Mix Never Been Cut': The Localized Production of Jamaican Music in Thailand." In *Asian Popular Culture: The Global (Dis)continuity*, edited by Anthony Y. H. Fung. Abingdon, Oxon: Routledge.

Shulich, Thomas. 2009. *Love in the Time of Money: Intimate and Economic Affiliations between Men in Chiangmai, Thailand*. Saarbrücken, Germany: Lap-Lambert Academic Publishing.

Sinnott, Megan J. 2004. *Toms and Dees: Transgender Identity and Female Same-Sex Relationships in Thailand*. Honolulu: University of Hawai'i Press.

Sinnott, Megan. 2013. "Dormitories and Other Queer Spaces: An Anthropology of Space, Gender and the Visibility of Female Homoeroticism in Thailand." *Feminist Studies* 39 (2): 333–56. https://doi.org/10.1353/fem.2013.0046.

Sklar, Deidre. 2001. *Dancing with the Virgin: Body and Faith in the Fiesta of the Tortugas, New Mexico*. Berkeley: University of California Press. Sprenger, Guido. 2016. "Dimensions of Animism in Southeast Asia." In *Animism in Southeast Asia*, edited by Kaj Århem and Guido Sprenger, 31–54. London: Routledge.

Srinivasan, Amrit. 1985. "Reform and Revival: The Devadasi and Her Dance." *Economic and Political Weekly* 20 (44): 1869–76. https://www.jstor.org/stable/4375001.

Srinivasan, Priya. 2011. *Sweating Saris: Indian Dance as Transnational Labor*. Philadelphia: Temple University Press.

Stewart, Kathleen. 2007. *Ordinary Affects*. Durham, NC: Duke University Press.

Stonington, Scott. 2020. *The Spirit Ambulance: Choreographing the End of Life in Thailand*. Vol. 49. Oakland: University of California Press.

Sunanta, Sirijit. 2014. "Thailand and the Global Intimate: Transnational Marriages, Health Tourism and Retirement Migration." *Max Planck Institute Working Paper* 14 (2). Max Planck Institute for the Study of Religious and Ethnic Diversity. http://pubman.mpdl.mpg.de/pubman/faces/viewItemOverviewPage.jsp?itemId=escidoc:2007856.

Suntikul, Wantanee. 2017. "Nostalgia-Motivated Thai Domestic Tourism at Amphawa, Thailand." *Asia Pacific Journal of Tourism Research* 22 (10): 1038–48.

Tan, Qian Hui. 2013. "Flirtatious Geographies: Clubs as Spaces for the Performance of Affective Heterosexualities." *Gender, Place and Culture: A Journal of Feminist Geography* 20 (6): 718–36. https://doi.org/10.1080/0966369X.2012.716403.

Tausig, Benjamin. 2014. "Neoliberalism's Moral Overtones: Music, Money, and Morality at Thailand's Red Shirt Protests." *Culture, Theory and Critique* 55 (2): 257–71. https://doi.org/10.1080/14735784.2014.899882.

Tausig, Benjamin. 2019. *Bangkok Is Ringing: Sound, Protest, and Constraint*. New York: Oxford University Press.

Tausig, Benjamin, and Tyrell Haberkorn. 2012. "Unspeakable Things." *Sensate: A Journal for Experiments in Critical Media Practice*. http://sensatejournal.com/2012/02/ben-tausig-and-tyrell-haberkorn-unspeakable-things-intro/.

Tsing, Anna Lowenhaupt. 2005. *Friction: An Ethnography of Global Connection*. Princeton, NJ: Princeton University Press.

Tsing, Anna Lowenhaupt. 2015. *The Mushroom at the End of the World: On the Possibility of Life in Capitalist Ruins*. Princeton, NJ: Princeton University Press.

Van Esterik, Penny. 2000. *Materializing Thailand*. Oxford: Berg.

Wadeecharoen, Wanida, Rungsun Lertnaisat, Somchai Lertpiromsuk, and Pard Teekasap. 2020. "Thailand Cultural Image and Destination Image through the Perception of British Tourists." *Journal of European Studies* 26 (2): 1–33. https://so02.tci-thaijo.org/index.php/jes/article/view/240601.

Williams, Raymond. 1997. *Marxism and literature*. Vol. 392. Oxford Paperbacks.

Wilson, Ara. 2004. *The Intimate Economies of Bangkok: Tomboys, Tycoons, and Avon Ladies in the Global City*. Berkeley: University of California Press.

Winichakul, Thongchai. 1994. *Siam Mapped: A History of the Geo-Body of a Nation*. Honolulu: University of Hawai'i Press.

Winichakul, Thongchai. 2000. "A Quest for 'Siwilai': A Geographical Discourse of Civilizational Thinking in Late Nineteenth and Early Twentieth-Century Siam." *Journal of Asian Studies* 59 (3): 528–49. https://doi.org/10.1017/S0021911800014327.

Wissinger, Elizabeth. 2007. "Modelling a Way of Life: Immaterial and Affective Labour in the Fashion Modelling Industry." *Ephemera* 7 (1): 250–69. https://ephemerajournal

.org/contribution/modelling-way-life-immaterial-and-affective-labour-fashion
-modelling-industry.

Wong, Deborah Anne. 2001. *Sounding the Center: History and Aesthetics in Thai Buddhist Performance*. Chicago: University of Chicago Press.

Yuval-Davis, Nira. 1997. *Gender & Nation*. London: Sage.

Index

Page numbers in italics denote figures, and endnotes are indicated by "n" followed by the endnote number.

Milton Keynes UK
Ingram Content Group UK Ltd.
UKHW012143120424
440953UK00003B/63

9 781501 774928